Building a Digital Repository Program
with Limited Resources

CHANDOS
INFORMATION PROFESSIONAL SERIES

Series Editor: Ruth Rikowski
(email: Rikowskigr@aol.com)

Chandos' new series of books are aimed at the busy information professional. They have been specially commissioned to provide the reader with an authoritative view of current thinking. They are designed to provide easy-to-read and (most importantly) practical coverage of topics that are of interest to librarians and other information professionals. If you would like a full listing of current and forthcoming titles, please visit our website **www.chandospublishing.com** or email info@chandospublishing.com or telephone number +44 (0) 1993 848726.

New authors: we are always pleased to receive ideas for new titles; if you would like to write a book for Chandos, please contact Dr Glyn Jones on email gjones@chandospublishing.com or telephone number +44 (0) 1993 848726.

Bulk orders: some organisations buy a number of copies of our books. If you are interested in doing this, we would be pleased to discuss a discount. Please contact info@chandospublishing.com or telephone number +44 (0) 1993 848726.

Building a Digital Repository Program with Limited Resources

ABBY CLOBRIDGE

Chandos Publishing

Oxford · Cambridge · New Delhi

Chandos Publishing (Oxford) Limited
TBAC Business Centre
Avenue 4
Station Lane
Witney
Oxford OX28 4BN
UK
Tel: +44 (0) 1993 848726 Fax: +44 (0) 1865 884448
Email: info@chandospublishing.com
www.chandospublishing.com

First published in Great Britain in 2010

ISBN:
978 1 84334 596 1

Typeset by RefineCatch Limited, Bungay, Suffolk
Printed in the UK and the USA

Contents

Contents

Contents

Foreword

David Del Testa, Ph.D.

In this volume, Abby Clobridge provides a roadmap for
the implementation of digital initiatives in the contemporary
information services environment of today's higher education
institutions. But that bland summary does not do justice to
what she has achieved here. Because of her long experience
bridging managers and technicians, faculty and librarians,
directors and assistants, Clobridge shows a mature sensitivity to
the particular needs of this moment of transition. The various
components that comprise higher education are experiencing
a wrenching period of transition in part encouraged, facilitated,
and in response to a concomitant digital revolution. Clobridge's
clear and complete plans for executing the design and
implementation of digital initiatives provide welcome guides to
projects for which the multiplicity of players utilizing easy-to-
use but still specialized technologies holds significant potential
for consternation and conflict. In this way, this text is in fact a
useful sociological or psychological commentary as well as a
technical or management guide, because the success of digital
initiatives depends heavily on the investment of their creators
in common goals and a cooperative rather than competitive
spirit. Presenting the interlocked dimensions of human control
and technical capability makes this volume more useful than
others like it.

Higher education has experienced a revolution because of
the technologies, systems, and technologists that have

become commonplace tools in the classroom, office, and laboratory of almost every college and university educator. Over the past ten years, inexpensive computers, near-universal access to the Internet, and the easy manipulation of digital images and sound have made what was once esoteric into the everyday, and what was once the realm of high priests of IT into practices and exchanges that have become expected and necessary for just about everyone. A single 64GB iPod Touch™ in 2010 has more internal memory that the combined storage capacity of the planet's computers in 1970! Through these tools and techniques, classrooms have come alive with sounds, images, and (usually) clarity unimaginable before, and usually beneficial to students. Humanists now regularly deploy as advanced users or experts high-powered geographical information systems to expose trends and associations in their work that remained hidden before. Social scientists have easy access via digital means to huge quantities of data that has made their work richer and more representational and nuanced than ever before. Hard scientists and engineers enhance their teaching in impressive ways through digital enhancement, and of course their research has benefitted enormously from the powerful investigative tools and methods of display now available. Librarians have played an increasingly important role in the implementation of these technologies at all levels, especially as the lines between libraries and centers of information technology dissolve. The future is exciting!

However, Clobridge reminds us that librarians must still know their pixels as much as their paper. Few people reject the utility of the new technologies and the enhanced access they give users, and they have encouraged a democratization of knowledge and learning unimaginable to even the most clairvoyant pedagogist of the past. On the other hand, not everyone has the same eagerness as others in making too brusque a transition from paper collections to digital ones, in particular with the concentration of knowledge in large, private, digital repositories for whom a bottom line remains the essence of continued existence. Those who illuminate the possibilities of the digital revolution and information democratization also have the power to turn those repositories off, alter their contents invisibly, and restrict through membership or technicality the information they have supposedly made available altruistically and expensively. Short of the pyres of Nazi Germany, for example, one cannot turn off a book so easily. Clobridge implicitly addresses this concern by encouraging sensitivity and perspective, for what's nifty to one person may be threatening to another.

Clobridge is not only providing her readers with a guide to the technical implementation of digital initiatives, but also a roadmap to its successful implementation within library staffs and between the library staffs and the constituencies that it serves, particularly faculty members. Library staffs themselves are undergoing important transitions from subject specialists and information catalogers to become a kind of digital locksmiths. Library users may gradually figure out the combination they need to access the kind, variety, and elements of information they seek, but smart users turn to librarians when they need expert sleuthing as well as appropriate information storage and safekeeping. The purview of librarians has thus remained concerned with as well as expanded far beyond traditional texts and traditional roles, and this expansion has caused tension between librarians and tough choices for managers who need existing staff to learn and implement new skills. Also, libraries remain repositories of subject-specific knowledge, whether in the form of paper or digital/digitized texts, and arguably an enormous need exists for librarians who have both a true subject specialty as well as technical skills. It has suddenly become difficult in new ways to be a librarian at a time when there is critical need for good, thoughtful librarians who can serve diverse and more or less ignorant constituencies excited by the possibilities they see around them but arrogant in prior practice or frightened by perceptions of potential professional obsolescence.

For their part, college students, perhaps naturally and especially traditional age students, have a strong sense of expertise relative to information acquisition, particularly using web-based applications. However, time and time again, research studies and critical self-evaluation have shown that students lack sufficient preparation to engage in mature and effective information retrieval through the now-universal computer interface (library catalogs, search engines, databases). Thus, as Clobridge illustrates, librarians must increasingly act as educators, and must, alone or in cooperation with others, construct teaching strategies that build long-term confidence and capability. The librarians become the interface for the interface, voter education advocates in the new digital democracy.

It is teaching faculty who perhaps need the greatest amount of convincing, support, and guidance of the kind that Clobridge illustrates here. Faculty serve as a bridge between the instant access of digital technologies and traditional methods, and they are often the ones to connect students with it as well, but they are not often literate in the new methodology. By the very nature of their profession, colleges educators, especially in the humanities but also in the social sciences and hard science, tend to have a conservative approach to innovations in communication, which is what the digital revolution is, fundamentally. Often trained in a paper environment, threatened by the fiscal crises that undermine the professorate and perceptions of a devalori-zation of both personal contact and learning without direct functional purpose, and under enormous time pressures merely to complete the tasks associated with their jobs (and exist as human beings), faculty members rarely have the time to keep tightly abreast of the latest innovations in instructional technologies. However, as Clobridge intimates, librarians and digital technologists should not presumptively conclude that faculty reluctance to engage in classroom innovation means that they have no interest in improving their teaching or the capabilities of their students. Far from it! Much like student users, faculty need education delivered in a (or multiple) manner(s). They need librarians to work with them, but they should also receive encouragement to incorporate librarians intimately into the classroom.

What is the moral of the story that Abby Clobridge tells? Librarians need to serve as leaders as well as followers, insisting on the implementation of those systems, technologies, and innovations critical to today's and tomorrow's library but retaining flexibility to respond to the needs and wants of the community they serve and to listen and respond carefully and sensitively to that community's concerns. Good planning, inclusiveness, shared perspectives, guidance, and most of all, clear, appropriate, and succinct communication will all ensure that a strong learning community develops and grows together from the library as the core of the higher education campus.

Preface

This book was written to provide a foundation for the umbrella of work tied to building a digital repository program. I intended it to serve as both a primer for new librarians and technologists starting out in digital repository work and as a handbook for those who are fully engaged in the field. I hope that it is useful for library directors, chief information officers (CIOs), and IT directors involved in strategic planning, staff development, and collaborative projects. For repository practitioners, it is intended as a mechanism to showcase current best practices as well as tips and tricks – both big and small – from institutions around the world. My objective was not to promote cutting-edge research, but rather to demonstrate how to develop a cohesive, sustainable digital program that meets the needs of its institution. I have emphasized planning, production, processes, policies, and models for efficiency in the hopes of helping others develop fiscally responsible, creative, and sustainable digital repository programs, collections, and services. Well-designed repository programs with realistic, quantifiable goals can help showcase libraries and knowledge centers in this era of shrinking budgets and an increasingly digital environment.

Chapter overview

In the introduction, I have summarized a set of guiding principles for developing (or shaping) a digital repository program. These guiding principles are referred to throughout the book, with additional points incorporated into individual sections (metadata, content recruitment, technical infrastructure, etc.). Part One of the book focuses on getting started. Chapter 1 is an introduction and background notes, a general introduction to the ideas of digital repositories, and some key definitions and how terms are used throughout this book. Chapter 2 covers strategic planning and is designed to be useful to those who are starting new programs from scratch, those who are shifting from isolated projects to an overarching program, administrators who are involved in strategic planning for the entire library, or practitioners moving to new roles or new institutions. Chapter 3 is a high-level overview of the technical environment in which repository teams work. It includes an overview of the systems and the infrastructure, including processing space, test servers, production environments, locally hosted systems, and vendor-hosted systems. It also includes strategies for dealing with more complex, real-life situations in a cost-effective way such as working with multiple systems and handling streaming video. Chapter 4 is an overview of staffing needs, including advisory/steering groups, roles needed to support a repository program on a day-to-day basis, and some ad hoc partnerships to establish.

The second part of the book focuses more on the long-term picture: building collections and sustaining the program, its content, and the community of support around it. Chapter 5 focuses on metadata: working with standards, developing your own schema, documenting information, and working in a distributed metadata environment. The chapter includes a workshop designed to introduce individuals to metadata production in a repository. Chapter 6 focuses on project proposals and implementation. It covers the basics of project planning and project management, specifically with regard to managing digital repository collections. Chapter 7 focuses on strategies to work with faculty and identifies other potential partners within an institution. It also suggests some easy, low-cost and no-cost ways to market collections after they are built. Chapter 8 looks at open access and the issues surrounding open access (OA) repositories. It clarifies some common misperceptions that faculty and the public may have about open access, and presents various strategies for supporting OA initiatives on campus – with or without an institutional open access mandate. Chapter 9 focuses on long-term sustainability: preserving digital objects themselves, identifying digital objects outside of the repository that should be considered in a digital preservation plan, sustaining collections, sustaining the repository team, and sustaining the repository program itself. Chapter 10 examines assessment techniques and how to gather and use meaningful data to make strategic decisions for a repository program. Chapter 11 suggests ways to integrate Web 2.0 technologies into repository work as a means of keeping users engaged and the interface look and feel current.

Perspective

This book was written from the perspective of a repository manager at an academic institution. When I started this writing project, I was working at Bucknell University, in Lewisburg, Pennsylvania. Bucknell is a mid-sized liberal arts institution with a merged library–IT department. I had the good fortune to work under the leadership of Gene Spencer and Nancy Dagle, both of whom were firmly committed to creating a digital library presence.

Since this project has been underway, I have moved to the Kennedy School of Government at Harvard University in

Cambridge, Massachusetts. The Harvard Kennedy School Library is a small part of a very large, decentralized library environment. The Harvard Kennedy School faculty passed an open access mandate in March of 2009, and we are in the early stages of depositing faculty, researcher, and student scholarship into the university's centralized repository, Digital Access to Scholarship at Harvard (DASH).

While these two institutions are vastly different, the principles discussed throughout the book have been applicable at both universities. I intended for them to be applicable at institutions of all shapes and sizes, including institutions outside of higher education. I hope that with a few small modifications (mainly those related to core constituencies and, to a lesser extent, staffing), the principles could easily be applied to other types of cultural heritage institutions such as museums or historical organizations.

Acknowledgements

I would like to acknowledge several individuals for their support and assistance throughout the project.

Nancy Dagle, Gene Spencer, and Mike Weaver: three of my mentors and those who supported my work to create a repository program. Nancy, Gene, and Mike all significantly influenced how I think about digital initiatives within academia – how to balance an institution's (or a faculty member's) needs with industry standards, how to take into consideration the unique culture of an institution, and how to create a program appropriate for the size, shape, and resources of that institution.

David Del Testa, my partner for several digital initiatives. David's abilities to develop creative, unusual projects and his willingness to experiment have resulted in several collaborations on both digital repository projects and projects to integrate information literacy into his courses. One particular project has been the World War II Poster Project, for which we won the 2009 ACRL Instruction Section Innovation Award.

Also at Bucknell University, Russ Dennis and Mike Toole, two faculty members who were early adopters even before we had a repository program in place; my original partners in repository work, Daniel Mancusi, then-digital projects technologist; Laura Riskedahl, then-metadata librarian; the instructional technology workgroup (Deborah Balducci, Mary Beth James, Leslie Harris); Jennifer Harper, our systems administrator; Dick Huff, our database administrator; Doris Dysinger, archivist; and Andrew Burnson.

At Harvard University, Kennedy School of Government, Steven Hoover, Leslie Donnell, and the rest of the Harvard Kennedy School Library.

At Chandos Publishing, Dr. Glyn Jones, Publisher.

Keely Wilczek, research assistant and librarian extraordinaire.

Last, my friends and family, particularly Mimi and Maury Krystel, Noah Krystel and my husband, Matthew.

Cambridge, Massachusetts
January 2010

List of figures

About the author

Abby Clobridge is currently the Associate Director, Research and Knowledge Services, at the Harvard University Kennedy School of Government Library. From 2003 to March 2009, she was the head of the digital library program at Bucknell University where she oversaw the university's digital asset management program, digitization projects, the institutional repository, and metadata production. During this time, she and her colleague, David Del Testa (Assistant Professor, Department of History, Bucknell University) won the 2009 ACRL Instruction Section Innovation Award for their development of the World War II Poster Project. Abby has over 10 years of experience working in library/information science. Prior to joining Bucknell, she worked at CNN as an investigative researcher and news librarian.

She can be reached at:
info@abbyclobridge.com.

Part One

Introduction

Right now, we are working at an exciting point in the history of libraries. External changes in the information landscape, technology, and users' behavior are all creating a vastly different environment from that of even five years ago. Digital repositories are one area in which we can apply traditional library expertise in an entirely new environment. Fundamentally, the work is the same: libraries collect, curate, disseminate, and preserve information. But in practical terms, the day-to-day work is vastly different, which has implications for staffing and resource allocation.

At academic institutions, one primary group of digital repository users is undergraduates. In general, undergraduate students are part of Generation Y – the Net Generation. While studies routinely show that students' in-depth technical skills are not as advanced as faculty hope or assume, students have grown up with the Internet, computers, high-quality graphics, and digital media. They came to college with expectations of one-stop shopping (Amazon), immediate acquisitions of digital media (iTunes downloads), and 24/7 access (the Internet is always open and can be accessed from anywhere). And so library services such as mediated interlibrary loan with multi-day wait periods and a lack of federated searching across article databases confound our users.

Opportunities for libraries

A digital repository program – and the services offered around it – is one area in which we have the potential to shine. It is an area in which librarians can demonstrate their value. Digital repository work gets the library out of the library – it enables us to interact with faculty and administrators in new ways and at different points in their workflow. For administrators, libraries can offer the skills and expertise of librarians to help collect and catalog information and digital objects that support the business needs of the institution and shifts the archival role of libraries from an analog to digital (or digital plus analog) environment.

A digital repository program can create new opportunities to support faculty teaching and scholarship. If a repository program is scoped out to include supporting teaching and learning initiatives, it has the potential to create new opportunities for partnerships to develop between faculty, repository staff, and instructional technologists. Faculty are increasingly teaching with digital objects (images, video, digitized text-based objects) and would benefit from assistance from library, repository, or instructional technology staff to identify, collect, and organize materials; teach students how to use digital objects for specific projects; develop new projects that utilize digital objects and emerging technologies; adapt existing projects to better utilize emerging technologies; collect, disseminate, and preserve digital objects they or their students create as a result of such projects.

On the research side, faculty members at many institutions who are early in their careers are running into a wall getting credit towards tenure for scholarly digital projects. The library is in an ideal position to be an advocate for this type of project and can help faculty showcase and disseminate their digital projects.

4

We can also serve as partners in the publishing process. By working with faculty from the earliest stages of a research project to when they are shopping proposals all the way through to the final stages of depositing completed manuscripts into repositories, the library is providing better service to faculty at their points of need. Plus, it allows us to have a much deeper understanding of faculty workflows. The University of Rochester has done a great deal of research examining faculty research behavior and what researchers want.[1] Now libraries need to apply this research to their own institutions so we can develop repository services that support existing faculty workflows and get scholarship deposited into the appropriate repositories.

Offering a set of services directly tied to the digital environment can be a way for the library to reach students as well, depending on the scope and focus of the repository program. Services can be designed to support the curriculum but also students' co-curricular lives. Some examples include:

- Student publications: collecting, cataloging, disseminating literary magazines, political publications, yearbooks, student newspapers.

- Electronic portfolios: teaching students how to create electronic portfolios, using repository systems to archive electronic portfolios.

- Workshops: offering instructional sessions on topics such as digital photography, working with digital images, editing digital video, finding and (legally) using music for video projects.

With shrinking budgets, it is paramount that libraries are able to demonstrate their value – and shift their services to add value in new ways.

Definitions

Below are definitions for some key phrases and terms. Some of these concepts are used in slightly different ways, so I am including definitions on how they will be used throughout this book.

Types of digital objects

Digital object: Any type of electronic file. Within the context of digital repositories, most often used to describe audio, video, images, or text-based documents.

Born-digital object: An electronic file or set of files comprising an object that was electronically created. Examples: a word processing file, an image captured by a digital camera.

Compound object: A set of electronic files and the structural relationship between them; all of these files together comprise a complete digital object. Example: the pages within a chapter within a book.

Digital surrogate: A digital version of an object, one that is intended to serve as a stand-in for the object itself. Most often used when referring to works of art. Example: a .JPG image of the *Mona Lisa*.

Types of digital projects

Digitization project: A project that includes migrating objects from an analog format to a digital format. Most often used to refer to scanning projects.

Digital project: A group of digital objects tied together by a consistent metadata schema. Can include born-digital objects or digitized materials, one type of digital object or several. Digital projects and digital collections are used interchangeably.

Metadata

Metadata: Technically, metadata is any data about data. Within the context of digital repositories, metadata refers to information about a digital object. Includes various types of details about an object including its usage and rights, descriptive information, and structural data. For further details and definitions, see Chapter 4, 'Metadata.'

Types of repositories

Digital asset management system (DAM): A system that can organize, store, and retrieve digital assets.

Institutional repository (IR): A library of digital objects and associated metadata from a single institution. The phrase 'institutional repository' is often used informally to differentiate between systems and services to collect and disseminate scholarly content (peer-reviewed articles written by faculty, electronic theses and dissertations) versus those systems and services supporting other types of digital objects (i.e., digital images of artwork).

Digital repository: A system that can organize, store, and retrieve digital assets. More specifically used within the library/ information science field than digital asset management systems. Within this context, it also incorporates the suite of services associated with the curation of digital objects such as digital preservation and ongoing metadata work.

Institutional repositories, digital projects, and digital repository programs

Clifford Lynch, in his 2003 paper, 'Institutional repositories: Essential infrastructure for scholarship in the digital age,' wrote:

> In my view, a university-based institutional repository is a set of services that a university offers to the members of its community for the management and dissemination of digital materials created by the institution and its community members. It is most essentially an organizational commitment to the stewardship of these digital materials, including long-term preservation where appropriate, as well as organization and access or distribution.[2]

While I agree with Lynch's definition, over the course of the past few years there has been an implication at many institutions that an institutional repository is one component of a larger puzzle. Specifically, IRs are often used to refer to the system (and its related services) that houses scholarship (faculty pre-prints, post-prints, data sets; electronic theses and dissertations; and, to a lesser extent, other forms of student scholarship) and does not include the rest of the services, systems, policies, procedures, processes, staffing and everything else necessary to support all facets of digital repositories supported at an institution.

To add to the complicated terrain, not all repositories are strictly 'institutional.' In increasing numbers, libraries are beginning to work through consortia, organizations of peer institutions, or with other local/regional institutions to deposit their materials in a shared repository rather than supporting their own systems. And in some disciplines, researchers are depositing their materials in subject-based repositories. The repository, arXiv.org, hosted at Cornell University, includes over half of a million scholarly items in physics and related quantitative mathematics and scientific fields.[3]

In hopes of avoiding confusion, I am using the phrase 'digital repository program' to describe the overarching set of services and systems that an institution provides to collect, curate, manage, store, disseminate, access, and preserve digital objects (although this does not include electronic journals licensed from database vendors). Furthermore, I would like to note a distinction between a series of isolated digital projects and a formalized program that ties together a cohesive set of collections and services.

Guiding principles

Following are some general, high-level guiding principles and strategies to keep in mind while thinking about your repository program.

- Align the program with institutional and library-wide strategic plans and initiatives. The program should reflect the needs of the primary constituents.

- Each institution is different. Every institution has its own culture, needs, and priorities. Create a program that fits that institution at that particular point in time.

- A repository program is not a static entity. It should change over time.

- Keep it simple. The easiest, simplest solution is usually the best. Don't overcomplicate processes. Don't try to shoehorn all needs and uses into one system.

- Don't let technology drive decisions. Use technology to streamline processes and solve problems, not drive policy decisions.

- Emphasize the idea of working in a production environment. Invest time and effort in developing processes that will support the bulk of objects in a collection, not the exceptions. Continually tweak workflows to improve efficiency.

- Aim for balance: focus on macro [program] level rather than micro [project or item] level – but find a balance between the two. Don't aim for the least common denominator and settle there – the collection will be unusable for everyone.

- Don't make it about the library. The repository program should be designed to serve the needs of the university as a whole. Generate interest from faculty, students, and administrators by starting with content from outside of the library.

Conclusion

Repository work is exciting and presents opportunities for academic libraries to support their faculty, staff, and students in new ways. It is at the core of the strategic direction we should be heading in as a profession. Our role is still to support the information lifecycle – creating, collecting, cataloging, curating, preserving information – but with digital repositories, we are able to support this work in a vastly different way.

Notes

1. Foster, N.F. and Gibbons, S. (2005). Understanding faculty to improve content recruitment for institutional repositories. *D-Lib Magazine*, **11**(1). Retrieved January 27, 2010 from http://www.dlib.org/dlib/january05/foster/01foster.html
2. Lynch, C. (2003). Institutional repositories: Essential infrastructure for scholarship in the digital age. *ARL: A Bimonthly Report*, no. **266** (February 2003). Retrieved January 27, 2010 from http://www.arl.org/bm~doc/br226ir .pdf
3. arXiv.org home page. Retrieved January 27, 2010 from http://www.arxiv.org. At the time of last reference, arXiv provided 'Open access to 584,317 e-prints in physics, mathematics, computer science, quantitative biology, quantitative finance and statistics.'

2

Strategic planning

The vision for a digital program

Since the mid-2000s, digital library projects have moved from being strictly the domain of large, research libraries to being integrated into academic libraries of all shapes, sizes, and budgets. What was once the domain of researchers and computer scientists is now being seen as a core function of many academic libraries. With shrinking budgets and the Googlization of the information landscape, digital repository work is becoming more central to libraries, not less.

The trick is to build a program in a meaningful way, one that directly serves the needs of your institution's core constituents while also being respectful of budgets and resources. I highly recommend investing a significant amount of time and effort in proper planning. Good planning will allow you to purposefully, carefully define your program. What is its scope? What needs is it designed to serve? What are its boundaries? What types of projects fall outside of this scope? How will you handle requests that are not manageable – either outside of the program's scope, not feasible in terms of resource allocation, have significant copyright issues, or simply are too costly? Having a well-crafted document laying out the vision for your program, addressing the collection policy, identifying what the program can (and won't) support will make it easier to explain decisions down the line.

While every institution has a great deal of objects ripe for digitizing or born-digital materials that could go into a collection, think about the overall collection, much like how we think about print collections in libraries. What is the purpose of the program and how does any particular set of content (or potential new project) fit into the overall collection?

Write a collection development policy to articulate what types of projects the program will support. Work with existing strategic planning documents: a strategic plan for the institution, one from the library, and one from the IT department. How do the objectives you are considering align with the strategic direction already set out for the institution?

If your institution has already built some collections, it is not too late to take a step back and conceptualize the program and document user needs, a mission statement, a collection development policy.

Strategic planning is not a linear process. Several key areas need to be evaluated, all of which can happen simultaneously:

- alignment with institutional and organizational strategic plans
- core constituencies' needs
- resources: staffing and budget
- infrastructure: systems, hardware, software
- content.

These evaluations should include some overlap in terms of personnel, but they do not need to all be conducted by the same person or group of people. However, if one individual is serving as the program coordinator, that person should lead this process. Ideally, a planning team will be commissioned, with a subset of members forming a working group. The planning team should comprise a combination of library and IT policy-makers, a systems administrator, other key members of the library staff (possibly including someone from special collections or university archives), and those who are most likely to be directly involved in the day-to-day digital repository work including a program coordinator. Faculty input is critical, although whether or not a faculty representative should be part of the planning team depends on the culture of your institution.

The working group should be an offshoot of this team and should be charged with most of the data gathering and document writing work associated with strategic planning. The planning team should have a kick-off meeting to discuss the upcoming process, goals and objectives, and assign roles and responsibilities to team members. As a whole, this group will be responsible for making big decisions such as defining the scope of the program, coming up with the basis of a mission statement, identifying individuals and groups to talk to throughout the user assessment process, and setting the overall direction for the planning process and ultimately, the digital program.

Without getting into details about budgets at this point, it is important to have some sense of the resources that will be available before working group team members begin discussions with members of the university community. Will there be enough support from the library to handle multiple projects per year or is the repository program going to be much smaller? It is imperative that those engaged in discussions with community members are not over promising.

This chapter is dedicated to strategic planning at the program level: gathering relevant data, assessing users' needs, articulating the mission and focus of a program, and bringing the right people together to make those decisions. In contrast, Chapter 6, 'Collection building: project proposals, planning, and implementation,' focuses on project-level planning and implementation.

Core constituencies' needs

Often a digital repository program is started because several specific needs have already been identified. Get input from all of the key stakeholders early in the process to be sure you develop a program that will meet their needs. Some typical stakeholders and potential projects are listed below.

Academic departments

- Art/art history department: transitioning from teaching with slides to teaching with digital images.
- Music department: store audio files used for teaching; collect and disseminate original compositions authored and performed by students.
- Department of education: lesson plans written by students, electronic portfolios necessary for students' teaching accreditation.
- Repository of learning objects created by faculty from across all disciplines.

Administrative departments

- Art gallery: creating a digital image collection to showcase selected items from the permanent collection to the general public; creating a database to store information about works of art owned by the gallery.
- Public relations: photographs used in various types of advertising materials – the university's website, calendars, mailings, formal solicitations, etc.
- Sports: photographs, videos of teams, individuals, and events.
- Data warehousing or electronic records management: supporting the business needs of an institution. Usually

not considered part of a digital repository program, although the two areas are closely related. The relationship between the two should be discussed if an institution has these services or programs or plans for such services.

Students

- Student publications: literary magazines, newspapers, and yearbooks. (Also of interest to alumni and development/ fundraising departments.)
- Theses and dissertations, masters papers, senior honors papers by undergraduates.

Faculty

- Open access repository of peer-reviewed articles.
- Support for new open access journals with faculty editors.
- University press publications.

Library and archives

- Often the library or an archive is the key player in some of the projects mentioned above. In other cases, this is a new opportunity for collaboration.
- Archive of born-digital objects related to the history of the institution: e-mail newsletters, faculty senate meeting minutes, committee meeting minutes, departmental newsletters, etc.
- Oral history projects.
- Historical photographs of the university.
- Mechanism to organize and present various miscellaneous items appearing at the library: student videos from a class, tapes/files of interviews.

Some of these groups are mentioned because they are policy-makers or departments that can potentially help a program gain momentum and support from the administration. Departments such as public relations/communications or athletics are often overlooked during the early stages of building a repository program, yet they can be valuable allies. These two departments usually generate thousands of photographs a month, many of which often eventually migrate to the university's archive. During the transition from print photographs to digital, this migration to the archives may have broken down. Plus, the quantity of photographs being generated each month has probably tremendously increased from the print photograph days. These departments are often quite eager to have some assistance from a repository team to learn how to better manage, catalog, store, and archive their materials.

Other groups listed are potentially sources of projects considered early on in repository planning stages. However, many of these are not necessarily ideal pilot projects. But while you are in the planning stages of your program, it is important to have a solid understanding of the breadth and scope of issues that your users need and the types of projects you will eventually need to consider. Start keeping a list of the project ideas that come up in conversations.

Users' needs assessment

Start by having conversations with key individuals whom you know will have a vested interest in the digital program – either as a likely user, a collection owner, or as an administrator or policy-maker. Then move on to get input through one-on-one dialogue, small group discussions, and survey data from a broader group of people.

For the conversations themselves, it is helpful to have teams of two involved in each conversation, one of whom has a solid understanding of repositories, and one who has a deep understanding of the politics and culture at that particular institution. One person should be identified in advance as a note-taker. Recap after the conversation to review and compare thoughts.

The strategies discussed below are intended to be primarily used to gather data assessing users' needs, but there are two additional benefits. First, by communicating with key stakeholders throughout the formal planning process, you are creating an opportunity for individuals to become aware, interested, and committed to the program early on in its existence. Even before a program has been started, you are selling an idea. Those whom you are consulting (as potential users or collection owners) become invested in the program, particularly if you are able to integrate some of their feedback in some way into the program. Second, by reaching out early in the planning stages, you might identify some unexpected potential early adopters, collection builders, and partners. These same methods are therefore recommended for content recruitment strategies.

Use these methods to gather quantitative and qualitative data and then analyze the results. Summarize the process, data, and analysis into a formal document that can be shared with others and will serve as a cornerstone for the strategic plan moving forward.

Peer-to-peer user groups

Invite faculty to a digital image users group meeting or a digital video users group meeting. Facilitate the discussion, but emphasize that the point is to get faculty talking to each other about their experiences. What are they doing with digital images (or video)? How are they using them to teach? What are they teaching their students about working with digital media? Have some questions prepared in advance to start a dialogue, but be prepared to let the conversation go in any natural direction. Faculty appreciate having an opportunity to learn from each other, and for the repository team, it can be beneficial to have a better understanding of what services faculty need, what kinds of digital objects they or their students are creating, and what kinds of opportunities this creates for the repository program. If possible, hold informal meetings such as this once a semester and create a listserv or blog to continue the dialogue between gatherings. See Figure 2.1, Sample invitation to video users' group and Figure 2.2, Sample agenda for digital images users' group discussion.

Figure 2.1 Sample invitation to video users' group

Dear Faculty,

As part of the transition to digital media at Langstroth University, faculty and students are relying more heavily on the use of digital video in teaching and learning. Desktop editing programs such as iMovie, Final Cut Pro, Sony Vegas, and Windows Movie Maker have made it possible for students and faculty to edit video on their desktops or in editing labs on campus. Inexpensive video cameras, phones and other cameras that can shoot video, along with easier-to-use and more widely accessible editing software have all led to innovative ways in which video is being used in teaching.

For example, in the Mathematics Department, introductory-level classes use video to supplement in-class activities. The department recognized that learning how to work through problems was a fundamental step in students' learning; the faculty responded by recording teaching assistants while they worked through problem sets and explained their work. The video is then posted to the course management system.

Join us to learn more about other ways faculty and students are using video. What kinds of projects are faculty assigning? What tools are available for you and your students? Listen to faculty share their experiences, and get new ideas you can adopt in your classes.

We hope to see you there.

Figure 2.2	Sample agenda for digital images users' group discussion

Welcome

Introductions: share with the group ways in which you are using or are considering using digital images in your classes or other reasons why you are at this meeting.

Other questions to discuss:

What assignments have you developed (or adopted) that use digital images?

How does the addition of a visual element enhance students' learning?

How do you encourage students to critically assess images?

Finding images: how do you (or your students) find images? Are you taking your own pictures, using images from databases, finding images on the Internet?

Do you encourage/allow/require students to use images in projects? What kinds of student projects use images?

What are some issues you have in using digital images?

Copyright: do you discuss appropriate use of images? Ethical use? Citing images?

What expectations do you have for students' citation of images? What guidance do you provide? What guidance could the library provide that would be helpful?

How can the library assist you in using images in your teaching, research, or students' work? If we were to offer workshops, what topics would be most useful?

At large universities, groups might need to be by area – humanities, social sciences, business and management, natural sciences, physical sciences, engineering, etc. The key is to invite large groups, not individuals. Don't limit invitations to likely users; you will learn a great deal from those with whom the repository team does not have a prior working relationship.

One caveat: keep the number of repository team members attending meetings low so you can emphasize that the point is for faculty to talk to each other – not the library/IT staff. It can be challenging to keep enthusiastic members of a team from attending, but it is worth the inconvenience.

Small group discussions

Facilitate small group discussions in much the same way as user groups. The key difference is that small group discussions are held with targeted groups of individuals who have similar interests. For instance, host a discussion for all art history faculty members to talk about their experiences transitioning from using slides to digital images.

Small group discussions can be much like a focus group, although a discussion led by the repository coordinator or a library administrator might be more useful than bringing in an outside focus group facilitator. Particularly when the objective is information gathering rather than program evaluation and assessment, it is not necessary to keep the core repository team members out of the discussion. In fact, it could be problematic.

Surveys

Surveys can be a useful way of gathering data from a large group of people at one time, although academic institutions tend to frequently survey their users, causing survey fatigue. If possible, incorporate questions related to the repository program's strategic planning to another survey – an annual library questionnaire or an annual instructional technology survey.

Start by determining what information you are trying to gather via the survey. Are you trying to determine how important certain types of services are? Looking for input on system requirements? Gauging interest from faculty or students or administrators about building new collections? How existing collections are used? How collections from other institutions are used? Looking for opportunities for new potential collections or partners?

After collecting data through the various mechanisms, document the key trends, patterns, and opportunities. The report can be a high-level overview and should be part of the strategic plan, but it is important to document the information that is gathered throughout these steps. See Figure 2.3, 'Users' needs assessment,' for a sample worksheet identifying sample projects.

Figure 2.3 Users' needs assessment: potential projects, known digital objects, and items to consider digitizing

Project	Contact/Dept.	Notes (size of collection, specs, timeframe, etc.)
Honeybees	Prof. Smith, Agriculture Dept.	Images and video, although might be interesting to scan some public domain texts as well. Potential for some grant funding. Collection should be publicly accessible.
Geology Collection	Dept. of Geology	Combination of topographic maps, digital images, and GIS data. Publicly accessible. Grant?
Athletics	Athletics Dept.	Photos and video of recent sports events. Some should go into the archive after a period of time; others should be restricted to PR/Athletics Department use.
Art History/Slide Library	Sarah Jones	Digital image collection from slide library. Copyright issues. Internal use. Library has committed to this project. Timeframe: FY12.

Internal resource audit: infrastructure, resources, content

In order to have a better understanding of what the library (and partners) can support, you need to know what you have and what you can easily and cheaply acquire. Buying a flatbed scanner is cheap, but trying to acquire Java programming skills can be expensive if you don't have someone in-house. Making an inventory of what you have will help provide a basis for making decisions about the scope of your program – what you can set out to do by mainly using existing resources.

The internal resource audit worksheets (Figure 2.4, 'Internal resource audit – staffing' and Figure 2.5, 'Internal

Figure 2.4 Internal resource audit: staffing

	Staff member	FTE	Notes (level of expertise)
Project manager			
Metadata (basic)			
Metadata (in-depth)			
Student workers			
Scanning			
Photo cleanup, color correction, etc.			
Quality control			
Copyright expertise			
Collection manager			
Liaisons: departments, centers, etc.			
Systems administrators			
Programmers			
Application admin (configuration)			
Graphic design skills			
Database admin			
Curator (description, describing)			
Content owner(s)			
Faculty partners			
XML coding			

| Figure 2.5 | Internal resource audit: hardware, software inventory |

		Have/need?	Cost	Notes
Workstations				
Scanners				
	Flatbed			
	Aerial			
	Black and white			
	Color			
	Book scanners			
Software				
	Photoshop			
	Picasa			
	Digital Asset Mgmt System (DAM)			
	XML editor			
Servers				
	Hosted on-site			
	Hosted off-site			
	Type of server			
	Type of database			
	Programming language expertise			
Storage				
	Locking cabinets			
	Secure spaces			
Storage: digital				
	Space			
	Network-accessible space			
Backup mechanism				
	Tapes (for server)			
	CDs (gold)			
	External hard drives			

resource audit – hardware, software inventory') are intended to serve as an inventory of existing resources. You may not need to use all of these resources, depending on how you define your program. But it is helpful to know what you have at your disposal and can be instrumental in crafting the mission of the program.

After completing the inventory, document the findings. Include notes about biggest obstacles and biggest strengths with existing resources and staff skill sets.

Legal issues

One last conversation to have as part of the strategic planning process is with someone from the university counsel's office. If the college or university has an attorney who is an intellectual property expert, seek out that person. Have a conversation about the digital repository program, some issues that you expect to arise in the future, and lay the groundwork for developing a working relationship with this person or the office. It is far easier to have an ally from this office when issues arise – and they inevitably will – if you have included him or her in conversations from the outset. Having support from the counsel's office can be invaluable. Make this connection as soon as possible.

Some typical issues:

- developing a non-exclusive author agreement;
- working with faculty on their rights as authors to obtain permission to deposit copies of their scholarship in the repository without violating copyright agreements;
- reformatting issues;
- drafting privacy permission statements;
- answering questions about music overlays in videos – what's fair use, classroom use, etc;

- helping to sort out who is responsible for objects in the repository if they accidentally include materials protected under copyright;

- out-of-date university-wide copyright policy that needs to be revised.

Determining what's realistic

After the conversations with users and policy-makers and internal resource audits have been completed, the planning team should regroup, analyze data, and begin discussions about what is reasonable within the existing institutional environment. The internal needs assessment is designed to raise issues that should be considered, specifically from the perspective of those who will be supporting the repository. See Figure 2.6, 'Questions for the planning group to consider,' and Figure 2.7, 'Sample completed internal needs assessment worksheet.'

Figure 2.6   Questions for the planning group to consider

Access levels: What kinds of access levels will the program support? Examples: personal collections, restricted-access collections (all internal), restricted-access collections (internal and external), internal-only (no further restrictions), on-campus versus off-campus, public access.

Long-term preservation: Will the program support all collections equally?

Metadata: Is the library taking on all metadata work or will this be part of the project proposal process?

Outsourcing reformatting: Does all work need to be done in-house or is the program amenable to outsourcing digitization and reformatting of files? If work is outsourced, who pays for it?

Oversight of the digital repository program: moving forward, will there be an advisory committee or steering group? If so, what authority does the repository program coordinator have and what decisions need to be made by the advisory committee? (See Chapter 5, "Staffing," for more details about steering groups.)

Figure 2.7 Sample completed internal needs assessment worksheet

Describe the anticipated short-term needs (within the next 12 months):

- Support for the National Institute of Health (NIH) Open Access Mandate among science faculty with NIH grant awards. Timeframe: NIH stipulations already in effect. Need services to support faculty as soon as possible.
- Database to store digital surrogates of objects owned by the art gallery and information about all of the objects (their provenance, value, appraisal, insurance). Timeframe: risk management office would like this database up and running as soon as possible.
- Electronic theses and dissertations: discussions have occurred in faculty senate meetings, but no timeframe has been decided. Likely within the next 6 to 18 months.

Describe the anticipated long-term needs, including identifying areas of potential concern:

2 to 5 years:

- The faculty senate is discussing a possible open access mandate. If passed, will need a place to deposit articles, services to support faculty through the deposit process, and services to support educating faculty on authors' rights.
- Increase in class-based digital projects. Would like to store these objects. Increase in requests from faculty to store students' work.
- Increase in requests from faculty for assistance to support storing and accessing datasets they need to use in their research and datasets they are creating as part of their research.
- Increase across the institution for support for portfolios to collect and measure students' progress throughout their academic careers.
- Infrastructure: workstations in use will need to be replaced. If scanning projects are approved, will need additional and specialized scanning and photography equipment. (Exact costs and specifications will depend on needs of individual projects.)

5 to 10 years:

- Digital preservation, long-term support for items stored in repository. Area of major concern.

As part of the internal resource audit, some big-picture decisions need to be made by the planning group, decisions that will ultimately shape the mission and direction of the repository program.

Shaping the program: writing a mission statement

After all of the data has been collected, analyze the information. Look for patterns and trends. Then draft a mission statement for the program. It should be brief and should highlight a few areas – but a good program is not designed to be everything to everyone. It needs a focus.

Some possibilities to focus on:

- Collecting and disseminating unique materials in a particular disciplinary area important to the institution.
- Collecting, curating, and disseminating the intellectual capital of the institution.
- Showcasing the scholarly output of faculty and students at the institution.
- Collecting and disseminating materials used by faculty and students to support teaching and learning.
- Supporting administrative needs.

Some key aspects to consider if you are working with limited resources:

- Don't worry about materials that can be digitized elsewhere. Several mass digitization projects are underway around the world such as the Google Book Project and the Million Books Project. Small-scale programs should focus on collecting and disseminating materials that are unique.

- Focusing on born-digital materials (rather than materials that need to be digitized) will allow limited resources to go much further.

- Who is the primary audience? If the primary audience is internal (students, faculty, administrative staff), you have more flexibility in regards to metadata – interoperability with standards and harvesting systems is less important. However, if the primary audience is the general public (i.e., if the objective is to broadly disseminate the institution's intellectual output), it is more critical that metadata is structured according to national/international standards such as Dublin Core (necessary for OAI harvesting).

- Use what you have: use existing workstations, equipment, systems, servers as much as possible. Take advantage of the existing infrastructure whenever possible.

- Use a project management approach to workflows. Have a sponsor, a project manager, and a project team. Use deadlines and milestones to ensure that projects move forward in an appropriate manner.

- Is the repository team going to serve as a drop-off scanning shop or will all digitization activities be tied to creating collections? Will you outsource scanning when possible? Scanning is expensive – it is more cost effective for the institution to send out large batches of scanning than to do it in-house.

- Is the repository team going to invest significant resources building personal collections for individual faculty members, collections that are not accessible by others? If the program is trying to focus on doing more with fewer resources, this is an area that can potentially cost a great deal with very little in return. Consider giving faculty tools to build and maintain their own personal collections but not take ownership of them. If the program goes this route, indicate it in the strategic planning documentation and later, in project proposal selection criteria.

At this point, you are ready to write a mission statement and a vision for the program. See Figure 2.8, 'Sample mission statement and vision document,' as an example.

Bigger than the repository program: aligning with institutional and organizational goals

Digital repository programs should be aligned with both institutional and library strategic plans. If not, it is difficult to justify their existence. Straightforward alignment does not guarantee success of a program, but it can go a long way in helping university policy-makers or high-level library/IT administrators see value in contributing departmental resources and staff time towards the program.

In order to ensure alignment, read through university strategic planning documents, identify areas where the program fits in or could contribute, and document this relationship. This information can then be conveyed in the formal strategic plan written for the digital repository program and included in presentations used to start discussions with core constituencies. It is a budget-friendly and strategic way to garner interest from administrators.

This step should not occur until the focus of the repository program has been defined as a mechanism to confirm that the focus of the program is indeed in line with the strategic directions of both the library and the university. You should review all strategic planning documentation early on in the process so the institution's direction is fresh in your mind

Figure 2.8 Sample mission statement and vision document

The Langstroth University Library will create a comprehensive digital repository program that will provide access, tools, and infrastructure to support the increasing number and variety of digital resources available. The digital library program will include content from a variety of sources: locally created digital objects, public domain materials, images licensed from vendors, and collections from other institutions.

The digital program will support the needs of the University at large. While individual collections will be created to support specific pedagogical or administrative needs, the program will be designed in such a way that leads to serendipitous discovery and the re-use of digital objects for multiple purposes. To encourage creating cross-functional collections, the digital program is built on collaboration – collaboration between individuals, departments, divisions, and other institutions.

The digital program will support projects that are tied to the University in the following ways:

Teaching and learning
- Create collections of digital objects that support pedagogy.
- Describe digital objects in ways that reflect the pedagogical intent of the collections.
- Support students' use of digital objects in courses and co-curricular projects.
- Foster an understanding among faculty, staff, and students of the intellectual property issues surrounding the use of digital objects.

Scholarship
- Facilitate storage of and access to born-digital objects, digital components of scholarship, and scholarly content in digital format.
- Support original scholarship of Langstroth University authors.

Preservation
- Facilitate preservation of rare, fragile, or delicate objects by providing access to digital surrogates.

Showcasing the university's unique digital assets
- Focus on materials that are distinctive to the University.

Share and collaborate
- Share collections with other institutions and make our digital materials available outside of the Langstroth community when appropriate.
- Explore opportunities to collaborate with other institutions to create digital collections.

throughout, but hold off on mapping the repository program's direction to the goals and objectives spelled out in institutional and library strategic plans until after you have evaluated potential needs and internal resources. Figure 2.9, 'Aligning repository program goals with university-wide strategic planning,' includes an example of how to write goals, objectives, and action items for a repository program that are tied to one of a university's strategic goals.

Figure 2.9 Aligning repository program goals with university-wide strategic planning

University's Strategic Goal: Expand Boundaries beyond Langstroth University.

Within the digital repository program:

Objective 1: Secure external funding to support projects.

Action Item 1: Apply for grant funding.

Action Item 2: Try to secure private funding from donors for specific digitization projects tied to the Langstroth University history and culture. Examples: digitizing the Langstroth daily newspaper. Work with Office of Alumni Relations and Development Office.

Objective 2: Collaborate with colleagues from other institutions.

Action Item 1: Host a regional conference related to digital repository issues.

Objective 3: Further dissemination of existing collections.

Action Item 1: Set up OAI harvesting of metadata for all public collections.

Action Item 2: Expand the scope/range of current projects such as the Honeybees Collection to include new materials solicited from outside of the immediate Langstroth community.

Action Item 3: Create and implement a marketing plan to support existing collections.

Action Item 4: Print and frame selected student-created digital objects to display in the library.

Putting it all together

The last step in the planning process should be to pull all of the notes together into one formal document. While it can be time consuming, in the long run it is worth the investment. The document should include an overview of the decision-making process and the plan for the program. If individuals who were responsible for large portions of the strategic planning process leave the institution, they aren't leaving with the entire institutional memory of the program. In addition, when new individuals are brought on board, either individuals who were not part of the planning process or who are new to the university, the document is an extremely valuable tool to bring individuals quickly up to speed. Figure 2.10, 'Sample outline for strategic plan,' is an outline for such a document.

Figure 2.10 Sample outline for strategic plan

Langstroth University's digital repository program

Executive summary

Mission statement

Vision
    Support teaching and learning
    Support scholarship
    Preserve materials
    Showcase the university's unique digital assets
    Share and collaborate

Background information
    The digital transition in higher education

Technical plans
    Technical infrastructure
    Discovery and access
    Preservation

Staffing plan
    Core program team
    Additional library and IT support
    Digital program steering group

Commitment to long-term sustainability of the program and digital collections

Goals and objectives: next 3–5 years

Appendix: supporting documents
    Users' needs assessment
    Potential projects
    Potential partners
    Internal resource audit: staffing
    Internal resource audit: hardware, software inventory
    Technical specifications
    Survey of peer institutions' digital programs

3

Technical overview

Introduction

This chapter is designed to provide a very high-level overview of the technical environment surrounding digital repositories. For a more in-depth look at the systems and components of digital libraries, consult *Digital libraries: Integrating content and systems.*[1] For a comparison of institutional repository systems, consult Raym Crow's *A guide to institutional repository software*[2] and Marion Prudlo's 'E-archiving: an overview of some repository management software tools.'[3] Charles W. Bailey Jr. has compiled a list of articles and texts about institutional repository software as part of his *Institutional repository bibliography.*[4]

Guiding principles

Overarching principles related to using technology to optimally support digital repository programs are listed below.

Use appropriate technology

Use systems that are appropriate for the level of complexity your institution can handle and the needs of the repository program. Make sure that the systems support mechanisms to extract data and objects into open formats, such as XML or CSV.

Needs should dictate system(s) in use

Define what purposes the program is going to support, then figure out the best (most efficient) way to support that need. Don't let technology decisions drive policy. Often, strictly using one system will not be ideal for accomplishing all of the program's goals.

Work within the existing technical infrastructure when possible

Be consistent with systems, languages, and equipment already in place. In much the same way that it is easier to manage five printers that use the same toner cartridge, it is easier to manage multiple identical scanners or multiple systems that all use the same type of database.

Use systems to aggregate content from multiple sources

It is not necessary to use one system for all purposes. End users don't need to know (and frankly, don't care) where an object is housed. It might make more sense to have the object stored in one system and have the repository point to another system.

Develop a close partnership with the institution's IT department

Work closely with IT departments. Take advantage of their expertise. Recognize what they can offer. Ask questions, and listen to answers. Have a solid understanding of the systems in use. Explain what you are trying to accomplish rather than telling them how to do their jobs.

Learn the difference between technology issues and policy and political issues

Often, technology is blamed for problems, when in fact the issues are related to personnel or historical turf battles. Be able to recognize the difference.

Use technology to simplify and to develop efficient processes

Learn how to create batch processes for all of your equipment and software – Photoshop, scanners, and Excel. You don't need to become a Perl scripting expert, but understand when something could be automated as a batch process and identify co-workers who can help.

General structure of a digital repository system

Digital repository systems, regardless of the specific software, are usually structured in a similar way. Most repositories are run on a relational database such as Oracle, Microsoft SQL, PostgresSQL, or MySQL. Within a relationship database, data is organized into tables, which have relationships linking them together. Oracle and Microsoft SQL are both proprietary systems that require licensing. MySQL and Postgres are open source systems and have become popular in recent years.

It is recommended that repositories are built on databases to ensure long-term flexibility and the functionality gained by not working with flat file structures. If you want to move your repository from one system to another, you need to be sure that the data can easily be extracted using a standard open format such as XML so data can then be imported into another system.

While the database is at the heart of a digital repository, the repository also needs to include software to retrieve information from the database, format it, and present it to the user in an easy-to-understand way. In a common deployment, the user interface is written in Java and made available to the user though the use of an Apache/Tomcat server. The application server may or may not be on the same server as the database – it depends on local practices. See Figure 3.1, 'Systems architecture,' for a diagram demonstrating the different systems involved.

The application includes mechanisms for administering the system such as handling user accounts and privileges, creating new collections, uploading/ingesting digital objects and metadata, configuring collections, and making collections available on their website. Once objects and metadata have been uploaded, they are stored on the server.

What digital repository systems do not include is storage space for digital objects and metadata while they are being 'processed.' This is an important distinction. If a repository program has several projects underway, it is likely that staff

Figure 3.1 Systems architecture

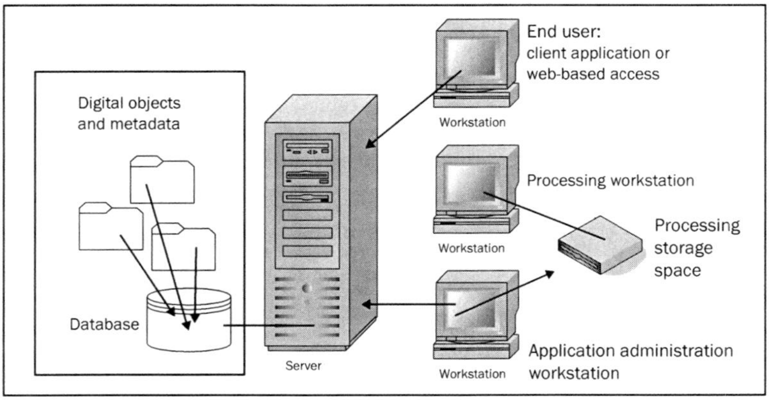

will need access to several gigabytes of space, ideally shared network space. If shared network space is not an option, consider using a network-attached storage (NAS) device in conjunction with cloud-based back-up storage. Inexpensive NAS devices such as Drobo[5] allow your staff to work from a central repository. Then, back up your files by using a low-cost, cloud-based service such as Carbonite, Mozy, or Amazon S3.

Production servers, test servers, and virtual servers

A general rule of thumb when supporting systems is to maintain at least two installations, one running on a test server and one running on a production server. The production server is the live system, one that end users access. The test installation is just that: an environment in which development and testing occurs. New software releases should be installed and tested somewhere other than in the production environment. Once a first level of testing is performed, test upgrades and developments in a test environment that includes all of the data from the repository.

One way to keep costs down is to use virtual machines – for both production and test servers. At an abstract level, a virtual machine is a fully operable server that exists in isolation on a physical (real) machine. A physical machine can host multiple virtual servers, which have no contact with each other. Such a set up allows the institution to support multiple installations of the repository system without needing to pay for the hardware costs of multiple servers or dealing with the space, heating, and cooling issues associated with running a physical server. By using virtual machines, a repository team could have access to multiple instances of its system:

- the production environment;

- a test environment supporting a current copy of the data from the production environment – used as a final point to test upgrades before installing and running in the production environment;

- a test environment with a small subset of data – used for development purposes and as a first point of testing upgrades.

Using virtual machines also allows an institution to use existing servers more efficiently: a single server could host multiple virtual machines running the repository system's production and test environments as well as other, totally unrelated systems. Most institutions are already using virtual servers; try to work within that existing environment.

Understanding the institutional environment

Even if you already have a system in place, repository owners should have a good understanding of the institutional environment – its infrastructure and preferences. Some questions to consider:

Institutional preferences

- Preference for vendor-licensed software? Open source? Open source with contracted support? Homegrown systems?

- Preference for locally hosted or vendor-hosted systems?

- Preference for a specific type of relational database? What in-house expertise exists? What types of databases are supported?

- What protocol is used for authentication – i.e., LDAP, Active Directory, RADIUS?
- Server preferences: hardware and operating systems?
- Backup methods? Frequency of backups?

If you are in the process of considering repository systems, some additional questions:

For the vendor

- Product support: what is the structure? Pay as you go? Pay for set-up support?
- Ongoing annual maintenance agreement costs?
- Is an annual maintenance fee included in the start-up cost or is there an additional charge for the first year of service?

Research questions

- Who is using this system?
- What are peer institutions using?

Locally hosted or vendor hosted

Institutions usually have a strong preference for systems that are locally hosted or vendor hosted, depending on available resources. There is no one right answer; each institution has its own environment, resources, staffing, and issues. Figure 3.2, 'Locally-hosted vs. vendor-hosted systems,' describes some advantages and disadvantages of each option.

If the institution does not already have equipment in place and available personnel, it usually will be faster and cheaper to get started if using a system hosted elsewhere. Over the long term, however, costs may even out.

Figure 3.2 Locally-hosted versus vendor-hosted systems

Type of hosting	Locally-hosted system	Vendor-hosted system
Advantages	▪ Digital objects are within a network, so faster processing times. ▪ May be able to take advantage of resources (hardware, software, personnel) already in place at institution. ▪ Closer working relationship with those responsible for servers and systems. ▪ More control, more flexibility – more opportunities for experimentation, for developing add-on functionality.	▪ Not responsible for hardware, software, or maintenance. ▪ System already in place – can lead to faster turnaround time for initial installation, configuration, and set-up. ▪ Often, can take advantage of consortia deals and gain access to a system for little to no extra cost. ▪ If working with multiple institutions, can be easier to manage if system is hosted at a neutral third-party site.
Disadvantages	▪ Requires systems administration personnel. ▪ Requires hardware/software – one-time purchase, ongoing annual maintenance costs, and regular replacements. ▪ Responsible for back-ups.	▪ Annual costs. ▪ More challenging to go from one system/vendor to another. ▪ Lack of control. ▪ Additional reliance on vendor. ▪ Uses expensive Internet or wide-area network (WAN) bandwidth. ▪ Potential issues with intellectual property being stored off site. ▪ Potential privacy issues if personal information about patrons is being collected/stored by the system.

Repository Systems

DSpace, Fedora, and ePrints

The repository market is becoming somewhat crowded, although most of the systems have a niche purpose. Three systems are particularly common at the international level: DSpace, Fedora, and ePrints. All of these systems are open source and are well suited for supporting work that would fall into the domain of institutional repositories – scholarly articles, student theses and dissertations, other types of documents. DSpace and ePrints are easy to set up and maintain. While they can support other types of media, their strengths are in institutional repositories. ePrints is particularly popular outside of the United States. While it bills itself as being an open source system, the development community is closed.

Fedora is a much more complex system and can handle all types of digital objects well, although it takes significantly more local development work and expertise. Fedora is truly middleware: it is a fully functioning architecture, but it does not come with much in the way of an administrative interface or a user interface. It is a highly complex system and does require a significant investment of resources (staff time and expertise) to customize. DSpace and ePrints are both designed to be usable out of the box, although DSpace also allows for significant customization if your institution desires.

Other systems

Greenstone and CONTENTdm are two systems with a particularly low barrier for entry. Greenstone is open source and is heavily used by institutions with very few resources because of its ease of use and simplicity to install and set up.

Minimal programming is necessary for basic implementation. It requires a server to host it and a local system administrator.

CONTENTdm is available throughout the United States via the Online Computer Library Center (OCLC) and is offered as a locally hosted application or as a vendor-hosted application. The vendor-hosted option is particularly appealing to many institutions. Several statewide and regional consortia include free access to CONTENTdm for a limited amount of digital objects. In these installations, customizations are minimal, but it is extremely easy to get up and running quickly and cheaply, particularly if your institution does not want to invest in supporting its own server for repository work.

Both of these systems are more traditional digital object repositories. They work well for digital images and scanning projects. On the other hand, neither of these systems is particularly well suited for institutional repository type work such as electronic theses or faculty scholarship. They are used by institutions of various shapes and sizes, often in conjunction with a second system for institutional repositories.

LUNA (was Luna Insight) is particularly strong at supporting digital images. Many members of the visual resource and museum communities originally adopted LUNA, but in recent years it has been used by several large medical schools and science organizations such as NASA. Several collections are publicly (and freely) available through the LUNA Commons website. LUNA offers locally hosted and vendor-hosted options.

A relatively new system, Omeka, was developed at George Mason University's New Media Center. Omeka is designed to be used with Dublin Core metadata to create web-based digital collections, primarily of images. It comes with several themes that can be easily customized, and it runs entirely on open source systems (Linux, MySQL, Apache). One item of note:

Omeka has a plugin that will easily allow for its integration into a Drupal website.

Several other systems exist as well. bePress and Digital Commons are two other highly used institutional repository systems. Many of the library OPAC vendors have their own systems, including DigiTool by Ex Libris. Several systems are ideally suited for museums or art collections, including Portfolio (by Extensis) and The Museum System and EmBARK by Gallery Systems. The Digital Library eXtension Service (DLXS) created at the University of Michigan is particularly useful for digitized, encoded text-based projects such as historical newspapers.

Working with multiple systems

One reason why there are so many repository systems is that no one system is ideal for all purposes. At most institutions, the most-commonly requested types of projects are: digital image collections, video collections, historical papers, open access scholarship, and personal collections of images or video. With digital image collections, users want to be able to manipulate the images, download them, see multiple images at one time to compare details, be able to zoom in and out, see metadata alongside of images. Users working with historical manuscripts share many of those needs, but they are also looking for easily searchable transcriptions of the text. Video files are extremely large in size. Users want to be able to start watching files instantly, not be forced to download large files. Open access scholarship lends itself to more traditional research-oriented functionality, similar to what users expect from Google Scholar or databases of articles. In addition to all of these publicly available collections, digital media is so pervasive that often individuals want to be able to manage their own collections of images and video.

While it can be cumbersome to support a vast number of systems, sometimes it makes sense not to force collections into a system that it is ill equipped to handle. The collections suffer, content owners get frustrated, and the collections are generally less used. However, there needs to be a balance between an unlimited number of one-purpose-use systems and supporting a few systems that together cover most needs.

Personal collections of images and video and Picasa

If your repository program is supporting personal collections, i.e., collections of images or video that a single faculty member or a small department want to collect, maintain, and control, consider using a system such as Google's Picasa. It allows a user to index his/her machine (or a shared server space), add tags to images, put images into folders, upload groups of images to websites that can be protected with a unique URL, and easily annotate web-based slideshows. Plenty of alternatives exist to Picasa, but it is free, easy to install and use, and works on PCs, Macs, and Linux. Picasa also includes some basic image editing functionality which keeps most users from needing additional software if they want to crop, rotate, and clean images. Most individuals can use it with minimal support from the repository team. It gives individuals a way to collect and organize images and video, make some annotations, and publish to web pages without taking away from repository work.

While this is not a formal digital repository system, it is still a viable option if you are strictly trying to build a personal digital image collection. It is important to match the tool with the purpose. Using a system like CONTENTdm for a highly restricted collection of images – especially one that the content owner should be responsible for maintaining – is not a cost-effective decision. Hosting personal collections on repository servers leads to more issues than simply the investment of repository staff time. Who is responsible for maintaining this collection if the owner leaves the institution? What sort of backup policy will the repository team provide for these collections? What is the lifespan of these collections?

The alternative – providing a simple, cheap tool specifically for personal collections – avoids most of these issues in a far more cost-effective way. Offer monthly workshops for targeted groups of individuals (i.e., faculty, administrative staff, support staff, faculty assistants). Give them the tools they need, some instruction to get them started, and serve as a resource if they need follow-up assistance.

Administrative collections

Administrative departments, specifically athletics and public relations, generate vast amounts of digital images (and increasingly, video). In some aspects, these media files are used in slightly different ways from digital objects in most repository collections. Specifically, media is heavily used for a short period of time early in its lifecycle, but then quickly gets filed away and is rarely if ever used again.

In general, these departments need to maintain a high level of control over their objects. Their work is focused on short-term processing and immediate use of the objects rather than long-term curation and preservation. If one of the purposes of the repository program is to identify, collect, and curate objects that are unique to the institution, these departments are often overlooked. If the repository team does not intervene, these images are usually lost altogether. They end up on discarded computer hard drives, disorganized external hard drives, or on CDs in drawers. In the pre-digital era, boxes of photographs would eventually make their way to the university's archives. The equivalent process in the digital era is often overlooked and can easily overwhelm an archivist. While there might have been a few hundred photographs taken at a particular event, that number has likely skyrocketed when photographers switched to using digital cameras. Now, that same event could easily generate a few thousand digital images, possibly from several photographers.

Managing digital images and video leads to the crux of the issue. Public relations and athletics departments are often extremely eager to have help managing the large quantity of objects they own. They need tools that allow them to easily manage their existing workflows, which are focused around supporting objects immediately after they are created – not necessarily systems that are designed to support the long-term lifecycle of digital objects.

Traditional digital asset management systems designed for the corporate sector (i.e., those that are focused more towards capturing and providing internal access to digital objects as they are created) are more ideally suited for this type of workflow than a repository system. Systems such as Canto Cumulus serve this niche. Systems that fit this need – that are designed to support internal, departmental workflows and not the dissemination of objects – are more appropriately financed by those departments.

If, however, the library is to play a key role in supporting such a system, it would be more appropriate to look for an alternative, either working in partnership with the IT department to create a homegrown database, using a network-accessible version of Picasa, or setting up a workflow productivity tool such as Adobe Lightroom in a way that can support multiple users.

Even if one of the repository systems is not selected as the primary home for working digital objects for these departments, the repository team should still work closely with these departments, particularly in regards to their metadata. If the metadata and its schema are structured in a useful way, the repository team or the IT department should be able to set up an automated feed from the departmental system directly into the repository. In this example, an athletics department's database includes the following fields:

- sport (basketball, volleyball, football, swimming, diving, etc.);
- level (varsity, junior varsity (JV), club, intermural);
- gender (men's, women's, co-ed);
- type of shot (close-up, official group, action, etc.);
- photographer;
- photo date;
- rights;
- status (send to repository, under consideration, N/A);
- names (name of individuals clearly visible in the image);
- description (free-text field for descriptive notes about the photograph);
- subjects;
- usage (website, calendar, alumni e-mail, etc.);
- usage date.

The repository team (and in particular, a metadata librarian) can be of assistance in a number of ways:

- Ensuring that the data schema is constructed in a meaningful way, one that will lend itself to the full range of the department's needs. Since metadata librarians and repository staff are familiar with a wide range of collections, it is likely that they will have some suggestions that might be helpful to the department.

- Work with the department to create a data dictionary that accurately reflects the fields and their formats, lists controlled vocabularies, and provides examples.

- Work with the department on a regular basis to review data in subject fields to ensure consistency.

- Map fields from the department's production database to the repository. Data from all fields should not automatically be imported into the repository. For instance, usage information, the cost of a particular photo, or what CD a photo was originally stored on probably should not be transferred into the repository.

- Set up an automated feed so that records with 'send to repository' selected in the status field are routinely copied out of the departmental production database and deposited into the repository system.

Even if the departmental databases are housed in different systems, the repository team should be involved in setting up the database and working to bring selected objects into the repository system. Getting the repository team out and involved in departmental work will further the visibility of the library and this workgroup.

Video

Video raises all sorts of issues for repositories. Video files are extremely large, particularly archival-quality files. Some repository programs have limited their acceptance of video files. While this may solve immediate issues, it is not a good long-term solution. As digital cameras are able to capture video, and cheaper video cameras are flooding the market, more and more people are creating video. Repository programs need to be able to support video in some capacity.

Institutions have several options for providing access to video to users in conjunction with storing an archival-quality file within a digital repository:[6]

- file downloads from a website or directly from within the repository;

- streaming video via a streaming media server;

- a hybrid version of the two using open source applications and servers;

- a hybrid version of the two plus off-site storage for 'streaming' files.

The first option, having users download a file from a website, is far from ideal although it is the simplest for repository owners. Put the video file (.avi, .mov, HTML5, etc.) on a web server or attach to a record within a repository in the same manner in which you would attach an image or document. Users click to download, and the file is copied over from the web server to the user's hard drive. After the file has finished downloading (which can take several hours if it is a large file), the user can then play the downloaded file through an application that is compatible with the file format of the video that was downloaded.

There are many problems with this scenario. End users are impatient and tend to want to watch video at the time they decide to download it. Waiting for several hours is not acceptable. Not all file formats are compatible with the most common video players: iTunes, for example, is not able to render all types of formats. Users tend to get frustrated if they have gone through the trouble of downloading a file but then can't watch it. Plus, the end user now has a complete copy of the video file.

Archival formats are totally incompatible with this scenario. Archival-quality files are simply too large for users to download, which leads to repositories storing two versions of each object: an archival version and a compressed version for users to download.

Offering the video through a streaming video server (Windows Media, QuickTime, Real, etc.) is an improvement in some ways. Setting up a Windows Media Server is easy and cheap – it is included as part of Window Server 2003/2008, which most institutions already own. The Windows Media Server user interface makes the process of converting source video to .wmv and then creating a publishing point to distribute the video quite straightforward and simple.

Unfortunately though, the files to be streamed must be in a format that is compatible with the server, i.e., Windows Media Video (.wmv) file format. Clients then must use a compatible version of Windows Media Player or VLC, an open source multimedia player that can support .wmv files. For end users running Windows, this set up works well. For Mac and Linux users, this set up is problematic.

One workaround solution that functions in a similar way to streaming but without the problems associated with being limited to using Windows-compatible formats is a hybrid approach using entirely open source solutions. In this approach, the video file sits on a web server, is encoded using an open-source transcoder, and then is served to end-users as Flash or HTML5. This process easily can be automated and integrated into repository work. Deposit the archival video files into the repository, use an FLV transcoder, and output the files as streaming flash video. This is not a pure streaming scenario because as flash video starts to play, it caches data to the user's local hard drive. The user's browser downloads bits of the file before it plays it. While the file is cached on a user's hard drive, it is not easily accessible. Sophisticated users can indeed download those files, but a user would need to actively seek out the file, unlike in the first scenario.

In this hybrid approach, the archival-quality file should be deposited in the repository, although the archived file does not need to be publicly accessible or downloadable to end users. In this case the repository is truly serving as an archive for uncompressed, original video files. In addition to the archive-quality files, the repository should include either a link to the streamed version of the video or, ideally, an embedded frame including the flash video, much like what users are accustomed to seeing in YouTube.

Considering the user perspective, in most cases users care more about how to access their files than where the object is housed. They want to be able to watch video immediately through their browsers, without needing to wait or install any specialized software. Users don't need to know where objects live, which creates more options for repository managers. Taking this hybrid approach one step further allows repository users to house the 'streaming'/flash video files off site in a system such as Akamai. If video is uploaded to an Akamai server instead of hosting it locally, the content is served by the Akamai server closest to that individual user. Akamai servers are located around the world, making it far faster and less bandwidth-intensive for users to watch video from wherever they are.

Using outside, inexpensive systems such as Akamai in conjunction with an institution's repository system and open source applications will allow for increased functionality, flexibility, and provide a better experience for end-users than working exclusively within the existing repository system.

Partnership with IT

Particularly for smaller institutions or any library without its own dedicated IT department, systems administrators, or network administrators, it is imperative that the repository team develop a close working relationship with the IT department. Digital repository work can present opportunities for the two units to work together and to develop a fruitful partnership. Repository work can create opportunities for programmers to use their skills in ways their jobs might not typically allow or present new challenges to solve. For the library staff, knowing who from an IT department can help with what types of issues can tremendously help. For example, if the IT department has expertise in Perl or Windows scripting, the repository staff can take advantage of this to assist with creating scripts to run various batch processes without needing to develop that skill themselves.

Keeping down costs

Technology is one area in particular where costs for hardware, software, support, and expertise can run a huge gamut. Make wise decisions, consider the existing infrastructure, think creatively, consider unusual possibilities, and take advantage of burgeoning open source communities.

Using open source

Running repository systems entirely on open source systems and applications is far easier than it was even a few years ago. Greenstone, Omeka, and DSpace are full-featured repository systems. With a simple installation, they work out of the box.

With a bit more customization, they can be tailored to match an institution's existing look and feel. There are several Linux distributions designed for server use, each of which includes a full suite of databases, tools, and administration utilities. On the web services side, Tomcat is often used to serve up Java programs, while Apache is used to serve up flat html files and run cgi scripts. Even if institutions are sticking with Windows and Mac operating systems, open source can easily be used to run most components necessary to support a repository program – including the repository system itself.

Hardware

To save money on hardware costs, consider sharing scanning equipment or splitting costs for high-end equipment with other library departments such as interlibrary loan. Look for deals on used aerial scanners or book scanners (which are particularly expensive) on eBay. Or make an executive decision that your institution will outsource any and all scanning projects that require specialized equipment. Meet colleagues at other regional institutions. If someone has just received a large grant that includes funds for purchasing new equipment, inquire about purchasing the machines that are about to be replaced. Work with companies who specialize in the buying and selling of used equipment. Search eBay for names of such companies, then contact them directly to see what they may have in their inventory. If you don't need an item immediately, let them try to find one for you that meets your specifications and budget. Or if you only need a certain type of equipment (i.e., a microfilm scanner) for one specific project, consider renting instead of buying.

Consider creative alternatives to standard problems. Tulane University in New Orleans is working on adopting plans that Daniel Reetz has posted on his website on how to build a book scanner for around $300 using two lights, two cameras, and a wood frame.[7] A similar scanner bought off the shelf would cost $10,000 or is available used for around $1,000. While high-end, specialized equipment may be better, keep in mind the objectives for your program. A consumer-grade scanner will probably be sufficient for most purposes.

Workstations do not need to be state of the art, but they do need to adequately function. While six-year-old computers may run, they will be using slower processors than newer machines. If you are using student labor to scan and the student employees are working on the oldest (and worst) machines, this means that scanning is happening on the slowest computers. Consider upgrading workstations or swapping the location of workstations so processes that would benefit from faster processors are run on machines that can handle the workload. In some instances, it pays to upgrade machines – or to invest in a second monitor or larger monitor so that the human time involved in processes can occur faster. At the least, make sure that your workstations are re-imaged regularly and are kept up-to-date with anti-virus software to keep the workstations as healthy as possible.

Batch processing

Nearly any task that happens in a routine way can be set up as a batch process, at least to some extent. Scanners that can handle batch processes can significantly speed up the time it takes to scan multiple items at one time, letting humans multi-task or work on another project altogether while multiple images are scanned. Various metadata tools allow for some typical processes (i.e., removing a leading article such as 'A' from the start of titles, extracting subject terms from a batch of data, etc.) Setting up batch processes within

Photoshop is simple. Tasks such as automatically rotating images, cropping them, and applying standard color correction techniques can be applied to an entire folder of images at once.

Learn how to master creating batch processing for hardware and software in order to waste less human time on redundant processes.

Conclusion

Remember that not all equipment (hardware and software) needs to be expensive. Look for creative solutions – finding used equipment, building your own scanners, taking advantage of consumer-grade electronics, using open source systems and software. Not all equipment needs to be state-of-the-art.

Work with others at your institution. Ask for help and invest time to create batch processes. Use technology to create solutions to your workflow challenges.

Most importantly, keep it simple. If your current infrastructure does not support something, look for easy, low-cost solutions rather than trying to force intricate workarounds.

Notes

1. Dahl, M., Banerjee K., and Spalti, M. (2006). *Digital libraries: Integrating content and systems*. London: Chandos Publishing.
2. Crow, R. (2004). *A guide to institutional repository software*. New York: Open Society Institute. Retrieved January 31, 2010 from http://www.soros.org/openaccess/pdf/OSI_Guide_to_Institutional_Repository_Software_v2.pdf
3. Prudlo, M. (2005). E-archiving: An overview of some repository management software tools. *Ariadne*, **43**. Retrieved January 31, 2010 from http://www.ariadne.ac.uk/issue43/prudlo/

4. Bailey, C.W. Jr. (2009) *Institutional repository bibliography.* Retrieved January 30, 2010 from http://www.digital-scholarship .org/irb/software.htm. Chapter 11, 'Institutional repository software,' includes texts related to institutional repository software in general, DSpace, Fedora, and other systems.
5. Drobo products web page. Retrieved January 30, 2010 from http://www.drobo.com/products/index.php
6. Smith, E. (2008). *Streaming multimedia for digital libraries and IRs such as DSpace: An introduction.* Retrieved January 30, 2010 from http://www.pskl.us/wp/?p=78
7. Ganapati, P. (2009). DIY book scanners turn your books into bytes. *Wired.* Retrieved January 30, 2010 from http://www .wired.com/gadgetlab/2009/12/diy-book-scanner/

4

Staffing

Assembling the team(s): staffing needs and considerations

Amidst concern about the future of academic libraries, digital repository work has been one of the few areas of growth. Library staff members tend to recognize this trend, so often there is an abundance of people who express interest in repository work. However, frequently there is a gap between what work is needed, what the work entails, and what resources (staff time, staff expertise) are available.

Many of the roles outlined in this chapter can be rolled into a few positions. At many institutions, it is likely that the bulk of the work described in this chapter will be handled by one, two, or three people. However, if the institution is flexible enough, additional staff members can easily be brought in to help with specific projects, provided someone focused on the repository program is handling the project management responsibilities.

Furthermore, each institution has a unique set of needs, culture, and history. The roles and tasks outlined in this chapter are meant to serve as a general guidepost that can be adapted based on an institution's needs.

Even so, a few staffing needs are consistent:

- repository program coordinator;
- repository planning group (for institutions just starting a new program);

- repository steering group;
- metadata librarian.

Digital repository program coordinator

Regardless of the size of the institution, it helps to have one person who is charged with overall responsibility for the digital program. Having one person coordinate a program will help lead to a cohesive, organized approach. It will facilitate communication within the library, between the library and IT, with content and collection owners, and with external constituencies. It will also help to create a structure that will lead to accountability.

Ultimately, the coordinator should be responsible for ensuring the success of the digital program as a whole; making sure that isolated projects, which may or may not be occurring simultaneously or with different team members, are progressing on schedule; that collection-based decisions are aligned with the program's strategic direction; that the program itself is evolving to assure continued alignment with the institution and the library. The coordinator should be responsible for assessing individual collections and measuring the success of implementation against defined objectives.

The coordinator's roles often juxtapose working with minutiae to big-picture vision and strategic planning. Responsibilities of the program coordinator might include tasks such as:

- Project management: serve as the project manager to build new collections; serve as the sponsor for other projects; delegate work; assign tasks; oversee day-to-day work performed by other staff members (who may not report directly to this position), student workers, or interns.
- Write reports: write project reports, end-of-year reports, grant reports.

- Assessment: assess long-term goals and objectives, gather quantitative and qualitative data, analyze data, and perform usability studies.
- Evaluate new technologies: stay abreast of developing technologies; recommend ways to integrate new technologies, services, and systems into digital repositories.
- Represent the library and the institution: talk to external constituencies, provide outreach to collection audiences, and reach out to potential content owners.
- Training: work with members of library staff and/or IT staff to train them on repository software, metadata production, and outreach activities.
- Ensure long-term sustainability of collections.
- Quality assurance: ensuring that tasks are being performed in a satisfactorily manner, checking in with content/collection owners to confirm they are satisfied with project progress.
- Provide guidance for digital preservation: refresh files, migrate file formats as they become obsolete.
- Grant management: writing grant proposals, serving as the principal investigator for awarded grants, writing and filing grant-related paperwork.
- Stay informed of changes in the national and international digital library landscape, standards, large projects, copyright issues.

Depending on the size and shape of the digital program and how many other people are involved in supporting repository work, a coordinator role does not need to be the exclusive focus of a person's job. Many repository coordinators also have more traditional librarian responsibilities such as reference, collection development, or instruction. See Figure 4.1, 'Digital repository coordinator job description,' for a sample.

Figure 4.1   Digital repository coordinator job description

Langstroth University is seeking an energetic, creative, and experienced person to coordinate our digital repository program. This person will lead strategic planning for the overall digital program, serve as project manager to build digital collections, and manage a team of librarians and programmers in the digital repository workgroup. The coordinator is responsible for all aspects of overseeing the digital repository program.

Duties:

- Manage the digital repository workgroup, budget, personnel, and projects.
- Work closely with other members of the library and IT staff such as systems administrators, technical services staff, special collections staff, archives staff, and instructional technologists.
- Serve as the resident expert on copyright and intellectual property issues related to repositories and digital objects.
- Lead the university's open access initiatives – supporting faculty throughout the publishing process, discussing implementation of a university-wide open access mandate to require faculty to deposit peer-reviewed scholarly articles into the university's repository, and supporting editors considering moving to an open access model.
- Explore and implement digital preservation strategies for repository content.
- Oversee marketing and outreach efforts for collections.
- Chair the Digital Repository Advisory Group.
- Oversee short-term planning and long-term strategic planning efforts. Identify new areas to explore, new technologies to implement, and new projects to pursue.
- Work with others to recruit funding and apply for external grants. Serve as principal investigator on grant proposals.
- Represent the digital program and the library on various library, university-wide, consortium, national and international committees.

Qualifications:

- Master's degree in library, information, or computer science.
- At least three years of experience working in digital repository development and project management.
- In-depth knowledge of digital repository best practices and standards; metadata standards and protocols; digitization standards and best practices; project management procedures.
- Excellent organizational, communication, and intrapersonal skills.

This position reports to the associate university librarian.

Digital program planning team

For institutions starting to create a repository program or those in the process of shifting from a framework of digital projects to a full program, forming a digital program planning group is a helpful step in getting organized. The ultimate responsibility of the planning team is to formulate and write a strategic plan for the repository program. The planning group should make all of the decisions surrounding the direction of the program and should include some high-level administrators from within the library who have significant decision-making authority. The program itself needs the full backing of the library's administration, which is why it is so important to have the library director or dean as part of the planning group.

Members of the planning team should include:

- the senior-most library administrator (director, dean, university librarian);
- the digital repository coordinator;
- a representative from instructional technology;
- one to two representatives from IT – administrator, application developer, business analyst, systems administrator, or database administrator;
- a metadata librarian;
- two to three other members of the library staff as appropriate, such as the library's senior technology manager, the assistant director or associate university librarian, a representative from special collections, a representation from the university's archives, a reference/ instruction librarian.

Try to keep the planning group small so decisions can be made and the group does not get bogged down in small details or logistics.

Working group: planning team subgroup

The planning team is responsible for making decisions and charting the strategic direction of the program, but often a subset of people will need to work together to gather data. This working group should include the digital repository coordinator and a few other individuals who can work with that person to interview potential repository users, analyze the internal environment, write reports, research systems, and compare what peer institutions are doing. Depending on the makeup and size of the planning group, it might be necessary to form a smaller working group in order to accomplish this work.

After the strategic plan has been written, the planning group has accomplished its objective and can disband. However, this group is a likely precursor to the digital program steering group, which may have a similar or identical committee makeup. For a full discussion about the work of the digital program planning group and strategic planning, see Chapter 2, 'Strategic Planning.'

Digital program steering group

Once a strategic plan is in place and the repository program is underway, form a digital program steering group. Even with a one-person program coordinator, it is beneficial to have a group of people to rely on to help make certain types of decisions – particularly those that are potentially political in nature. The purpose of the steering group is mainly to review project proposals, allocate resources, and plan for the long term. The steering group should be involved in any potential grant applications and be aware of discussions for potential sources of external funding.

If the program is accepting proposals from content owners, the steering group needs to carefully review applications and decide which projects to approve. The steering group needs to weigh the merits of the proposal, the working relationship between the library and the proposer, resource allocation of repository staff, and long-term implications for storage and preservation of the collection. Are there political issues that need to be considered? At some institutions, pre-tenured faculty are discouraged from embarking on digital projects to support their teaching or research. If this is the case, are there implications for the library if a particular proposal is accepted? This is just one example. See Chapter 6, 'Collection building' for more details on the proposal and review projects. The process of deciding whether or not to move forward with a project can be controversial and needs the backing and commitment of the organization to ensure long-term sustainability. Getting the right players involved in the decision-making process is helpful.

Ideally, a steering group includes:

- digital repository program coordinator;
- library administrator(s);
- an instructional technologist, if appropriate based on the needs of the program;
- an IT administrator;
- metadata librarian;
- additional representative(s) from the library.

Including additional members of the library staff on a rotating basis for a set length of time (one year) can be a good way to include other librarians in repository work. However, groups should be limited to a small number of people.

An alternative to creating a new committee within the library is to use an existing advisory group. Many libraries

67

have upper-level management teams who vet decisions with significant resource implications. If a senior-level management team from within the library is to take on this role, the person coordinating the digital program should be included in these discussions if that person is not usually part of such a team.

Project teams

Once a project has been approved and it is underway, the steering group moves out of the way and the project is passed along to a project team. Teams should be created based on the specific needs of a project and corresponding skills of the staff members. Teams usually consist of:

- project manager;

- metadata librarian;

- additional staff, student employees as appropriate, based on the needs of the project.

Teams usually vary in size based on the scope, breadth, and size of projects. For example, a small, straightforward project can be accomplished with a small team. More complex projects can take months or years and several staff members to complete.

In order to keep projects moving forward without using vast quantities of resources, carefully consider proposals. See Chapter 6 for further details on the project management and implementation.

Metadata team

Metadata is a key aspect of every digital project and requires widely varying sets of skills and expertise. Much of the work requires a great deal of expertise but other work is extremely straightforward and not terribly technical. Metadata needs to be assigned to each field for each record for each object. Ideally, the library will have a dedicated metadata librarian – or several metadata librarians.

Typical responsibilities of a metadata librarian

- defining metadata schemas for collections;
- working with standards and subject thesauri;
- writing data dictionaries;
- preparing the collection for Open Archives Initiatives (OAI) harvesting.

Other metadata work

- long-term authority control within a collection;
- authority control work between collections;
- cleanup work.

See Chapter 5, 'Metadata' for a complete discussion of the range of metadata work associated with digital repositories. See Figure 4.2, 'Metadata librarian job description,' for a sample posting.

Technical/infrastructure team

The shape, size, and configuration of the technical/ infrastructure team will depend on the systems being used and whether the systems are locally hosted (i.e., sitting on a server at your institution) or hosting will happen off site and another organization will be responsible for it. For an overview of

Figure 4.2   Metadata librarian job description

The metadata librarian manages and coordinates activities related to metadata production and curation for Langstroth University's digital collections.

S/he is responsible for the intellectual access to Langstroth's digital collections, ensuring that users are able to find and retrieve materials, making recommendations for improving the intellectual access to digital objects, and implementing such changes. This individual will be responsible for metadata and associated authority control, quality control, knowledge of changing metadata standards, and other duties associated with the creation and maintenance of data related to digital materials.

The metadata librarian is part of the digital repository workgroup and will report to the digital repository coordinator.

Primary responsibilities include:

- Maintaining knowledge of national and international descriptive, technical, and administrative metadata standards. Interpreting and adapting those standards for local needs.
- Selecting the appropriate metadata scheme for digital projects.
- Coordinating the creation of metadata and long-term maintenance of data for projects. Working with faculty, staff, students, and administrators to establish and implement best practices for individual collections.
- Establishing workflows for metadata projects. Coordinating metadata work assigned to other staff and student workers. Overseeing training on related software and tasks.
- Experimenting with promising new metadata/cataloging tools or technologies. Developing strategies for integrating new technologies and services into the existing framework.
- Seeking to create more efficient workflows for data creation, manipulation, cleanup and storage. Exploring, recommending, and implementing processes to automate work.
- Participating in training campus users on digital object storage, presentation, and cataloging software.
- Anticipating future trends in an evolving digital environment. Maintaining current awareness of national and international developments affecting metadata, cataloging, and information retrieval. Attending professional meetings and workshops to monitor changes in metadata standards and practices.
- Represent the workgroup by serving on university-wide, departmental, and consortial committees as appropriate.

> **Qualifications**
> - Master's degree in library science or information science.
> - Knowledge of existing and developing metadata schemas, standards, and protocols such as Dublin Core, VRA Core, LOM, MODS, METS, CCO, and OAI-PMH; traditional cataloging rules and standards including MARC and AACR2; subject thesauri such as LCSH, ULAN, AAT, TGN, and MeSH; emerging standards such as RDA.
> - Ability to adapt to changing digital technologies and metadata standards.
> - Proficiency in standard computer applications, spreadsheets, databases, integrated library systems, the Internet, as well as traditional library resources.
> - The ability to learn new systems and procedures quickly.
> - Excellent written and oral communication skills.
> - The ability to work independently, with minimal supervision, and in teams.

digital repository systems, the technical environment, and roles of the technical team see Chapter 3, 'Technical overview.'

For institutions hosting their own digital repository systems, there are a number of roles that will be required including a systems administrator, database administrator, and application administrator. Additionally, it is helpful to be in contact with a programmer and a network administrator.

System and database administrators

System administrators are responsible for setting up the servers on which systems are installed. They often manage a production installation and a test installation for each system. The system administrator oversees installation, day-to-day-management, backups, and user privileges.

At a larger institution, the repository team might have their own system administrator. Otherwise, the system administrator might be from the IT department. If this is the case, the system administrator also usually serves as the main liaison to the IT department.

Some institutions have separate, dedicated database administration groups. If this is the case, a member of that team would work with the system administrator to install and configure the database underlying the repository and backup the database itself. One person may be responsible for the system and the database, or it might depend on what kind of database is in use.

An important item to discuss with system and database administrators is backups. How often are backups captured? What format? Have you tested the process to recover data from a backup?

Application administrator(s)

In addition to managing the system itself, someone needs to be responsible for the application to handle customizations of the software. Ideally, this will be a member of the repository team. This person needs a high level of technical understanding, although he or she does not need to be a programmer. He/she should be comfortable working with administrative interfaces of applications.

The application administrator also needs to coordinate user accounts. Even if collections are generally accessible to the entire campus community, the repository might have the ability to create individual accounts. The repository team does not want to get into the business of creating unique, local accounts for every member of the campus community. Work with others to tie repository accounts to existing methods of authentication (whether or not a user has access to a collection) and authorization (the level of privileges and permissions an individual user has to a particular collection).

The look and feel of collections is another area of responsibility that usually falls to the application administrator. How does a collection look? Is it consistent with other collections? Is it consistent with other campus systems or the university's website? Should it be consistent or should it have its own brand?

Programmers

Some part-time, project-based programming assistance can be useful to develop automated processes. For instance, a programmer could write macros for spreadsheet software to automate consistent processes in metadata work. A programmer could also be helpful in developing ways to feed data from one system into another system.

In an ideal configuration, the repository workgroup will combine the responsibilities of application administrators and programmers into one dedicated position. See Figure 4.3, 'Digital project technologist job description,' for a sample job description for such a position.

Network administrator

Since digital objects usually require large amounts of storage space and are bandwidth-intensive to move across networks, it is helpful to work with a network administrator. Network administrators can be particularly helpful in working with digital video.

Instructional technologists

For programs that emphasize supporting the use of digital objects within the curriculum or for teaching, instructional technologists are a natural partner. Instructional technologists are already working closely with faculty and supporting

Figure 4.3   Digital projects technologist job description

Langstroth University is seeking a digital projects technologist who will work to enhance access to the University's digital assets and will play a key role in expanding our digital collections. The primary responsibilities will be to prepare digital objects for production; create or enhance metadata for digital objects; create tools to improve workflows; and provide quality control for the work of students, staff, and vendors.

This position will be part of the digital repository workgroup and will work closely with staff from various workgroups within the library and IT.

Duties:

- Assist with application administration for digital object storage and delivery systems such as ePrints, DSpace, Fedora, and CONTENTdm. Assist with training staff, faculty, and students for these systems. Assist with troubleshooting and software upgrades.
- Identify, evaluate, recommend, and implement tools used to improve efficiency and accuracy for digital object and metadata production processes.
- Work directly with faculty and staff to build digital object collections.
- Assist with outreach efforts to increase off-campus usage of collections.
- Maintain the digital repository program's web presence on the library website and all external sites such as Flickr and Twitter.
- Experiment with emerging technologies related to digital imaging and web standards.
- Follow various sets of rules to create, enhance, and standardize data related to digital objects.
- Identify sources for authority and perform research related to newly acquired digital images.
- Write scripts for processing digital objects.
- Provide quality control and authority for work on digital projects.
- Produce documentation for best practices for tasks such as scanning, image cleanup, and OCR.
- Represent the workgroup and repository program on library, IT, campus, and external committees.
- Additional responsibilities will be based on interests, knowledge, and experience.

Required qualifications, experience, and skills:

- Bachelor's degree.
- Proficiency with Mac and PC operating systems and network-based resources.
- Experience working with digital objects (images, audio, video, and text).
- Experience with scripting languages.
- Proficiency with Excel.
- Detail oriented.
- Ability to communicate effectively (written and oral) and to work collaboratively.
- Ability to work with minimal supervision.
- Ability to manage priorities, juggle multiple projects at once, and complete assigned tasks and projects on time.
- An interest in metadata and digital library standards and best practices.
- Preferred: familiarity with subject access, authority control, thesauri, and online library systems; familiarity with copyright and fair use; experience with digital library applications.

their use of digital media. Invite a member of the instructional technologist team to be part of the repository planning group and the repository steering group. Ask for input on potential partners. Invite them to join you at meetings with faculty. Have them participate in outreach activities for the repository program.

Instructional technologists, librarians, and the repository team can work together to share responsibilities for working with faculty:

- leading workshops on how to organize and collect images in personal collections;

- using Flickr and Picasa;

- working with licensed databases of images (ARTstor, AP Accunet);

- finding and using Creative Commons images and public domain images.

Partnering with instructional technologists for digital repository work can be beneficial for the repository team, instructional technologists, and faculty.

Getting IT staff involved in repository work

While there are clear reasons to get IT staff involved in repository work, sometimes it can be challenging to get your foot in the door. A few suggestions to generate interest: host an open house for the repository program, give a presentation to library and IT staff talking about the strategic planning process, host a metadata training workshop, or simply invite selected individuals to participate in projects.

Librarians and repository work

Some institutions are starting to shift or expand job responsibilities so that all librarians are involved in some aspect of institutional repository work, most often outreach work. In order for this dynamic to be effective, librarians need to fully understand the repository program at their institution. Specifically, they need to understand what is possible so they do not unwittingly over promise something to faculty. The University of Minnesota is one such library that is incorporating scholarly communication roles into academic librarian position descriptions. Kara Malenfant in her article, 'Leading change in the system of scholarly communication: A case study of engaging liaison librarians for outreach to faculty,'[1] examines the University of Minnesota model. Tyler Walters, in 'Reinventing the library – how repositories are causing librarians to rethink their professional roles,' also examines how librarians are shifting their roles within this context.[2]

Librarian for scholarly communication

Rather than having all librarians become involved in repository work, more institutions are starting to dedicate a position to coordinating open access initiatives, scholarly communication, or digital scholarship. This person tends to focus more on working directly with the faculty as a partner in the publishing process rather than focusing on the technical work of repositories.

Digital repository workgroups

Much discussion has taken place in academic libraries about where within the organizational structure repository work should live. Some institutions have put repository teams together into their own workgroup. Even if it is a small workgroup of two to three individuals, it allows team members to focus on their work and not get pulled into too many different directions or unrelated projects. In this framework, the workgroup usually consists of a repository coordinator plus a few other technical staff members, student assistants, and possibly a library science intern; or, the group consists of the repository coordinator, a metadata librarian, one to two additional team members (a programmer or systems administrator, or a junior librarian), student assistants, and possibly a library science intern. This scenario is ideal to support repository work, even if the repository staff members also have additional responsibilities such as instruction, reference, or collection development.

The alternatives to having a stand-alone repository workgroup are including the repository team in technical services, public services, or special collections/archives. All of these models are common. But since each institution has its own culture, what works at one institution might not work as well in another environment. If the institution can be flexible, get creative and try some different configurations. For example, at the University of Richmond, the Digital Initiatives Group is responsible for digital repository work plus scanning of items for electronic reserves and interlibrary loan.[3]

Library and information science interns

Hiring library/information science interns can help to grow the repository team and can provide valuable real-world experience to graduate students. In most instances, internships work out extremely well for both the interns and the library. Check with your institution about policies governing internships.

It is most cost-effective to offer unpaid internships in exchange for course credit, but not all universities will allow unpaid internships. Library and information science (LIS) programs usually have a set of rules governing for-credit internships. Students often need to write a paper about the internship, their supervisor needs to write a formal review, and an agreed set of learning objectives might need to be negotiated at the start of the internship. While this type of internship involves a fair amount of paperwork, it can be an excellent development opportunity for a staff member who does not already have formal supervisory experience.

The other option is a paid internship, which is similar to hiring a student worker. However, by calling the job an internship and integrating learning opportunities into the position, the job itself becomes much more appealing. Market it specifically to LIS graduate students. The position can be shaped in various ways, depending on the needs of the library: a digital library internship, metadata internship, or an open access internship.

See Figure 4.4, 'Intern job description,' for an example and Figure 4.5, 'Intern learning objectives,' for further details.

Figure 4.4   Intern job description

Langstroth University is offering a paid summer internship for a library/information science student interested in learning more about digital libraries. This position is designed to provide experience in all aspects of an academic digital library/technology environment. Responsibilities will include (but not be limited to) assisting with digital image processing, metadata work, and other tasks associated with building a digital collection. During the upcoming summer, the digital repository workgroup will be building three digital image collections: Honeybees, University History, and Art & Art History. These collections will be used to support courses. There will be opportunities for hands-on experience in a variety of areas.

Requirements:
- Applicants must be currently enrolled in a library, information science, or related degree program.
- Knowledge of metadata standards and/or experience with digital image software such as Photoshop would be helpful but is not required.
- Interns must be willing to work a minimum of 25 hours per week.

Figure 4.5   Intern learning objectives

Work tasks:

1. Image processing and maintenance
   - scanning
   - image cleanup
   - de-screening
   - color correction
   - quality control
   - long-term preservation
   - archival work of digital images

2. Data
   - Follow rules and guidelines using Excel to automate and clean up data from vendors to fit local needs.
   - Help prepare locally created materials for open access harvesting (OAI-PMH).
   - Use thesauri (TGN, ULAN, AAT, LCSH, MeSH).
   - Create metadata for three collections: Honeybees, University History, and Art & Art History.

Associated learning objectives:

- Understand metadata standards, why they are used, and limitations within pedagogical realm.
- Understand end-user behavior for digital collections in an academic environment.
- Understand preservation methods used in digital asset management and issues involved in long-term storage of digital assets.
- Understand copyright issues involved in providing access to art images.
- Understand metadata and its relationship to database searching.
- Understand how the purpose of the project affects how the collection is built.
- Understand different rationales for embarking on digitization projects – disseminating unique university materials, preservation of originals, increased access, storing born-digital materials, etc.

Notes

1. Malenfant, K. (2010). Leading change in the system of scholarly communication: A case study of engaging liaison librarians for outreach to faculty. *College & Research Libraries*, 71, 63–76.
2. Walters, T. (2007). Reinventing the library – how repositories are causing librarians to rethink their professional roles. *portal: Libraries and the Academy*, 7(2), 213–225.
3. University of Richmond (n.d.). *Digital initiatives*. Retrieved January 30, 2010 from http://library.richmond.edu/digital/index.html

Part Two

5

Metadata

What is metadata?

Metadata, at its most basic level, is 'data about data.' Metadata should be structured, organized information about an object such as its source, scope, physical or digital characteristics, context, or any other details about the object itself. It applies to both physical (analog) and digital objects:

- Metadata in books: Title, author, ISBN, call number. See Figure 5.1, 'MARC metadata.'

- Metadata in web pages: keywords, title, author, software, version. See Figure 5.2, 'Metadata in HTML.'

- Metadata associated with digital images or video: data of photograph, camera, GIS coordinates, subjects, photographer. See Figure 5.3, 'Metadata in images or video.'

- Metadata in word processing documents: author, date of creation, software version. See Figure 5.4, 'Metadata in word processing documents.'

While data within library catalogs is indeed a type of metadata, the library community typically refers to the set of processes related to describing books and serials within MARC using AACR2 as 'cataloging.' Metadata, on the other hand, is conventionally used to differentiate between this work and the processes associated with describing digital objects.

Figure 5.1 MARC metadata

Metadata in human-readable format from library catalog record for *Using Honey Bees to Pollinate Crops*:

LC Control No.:	agr68000286
LCCN Permalink:	http://lccn.loc.gov/agr68000286
Type of Material:	Book (Print, Microform, Electronic, etc.)
Corporate Name:	United States. Entomology Research Service.
Main Title:	Using honey bees to pollinate crops.
Published/Created:	[Washington, U.S. Govt. Print. Off., 1968]
Description:	7 p. illus. 24 cm.
Subjects:	Honeybee.
	Pollination by insects.
	Fertilization of plants by insects.
	Apis mellifera.
Series:	United States. Dept. of Agriculture. Leaflet no. 549
	Leaflet (United States. Dept. of Agriculture); no. 549.
LC Classification:	S21 .A483 no. 549
NAL Class No.:	1 Ag84L no. 549

MARC Metadata from Library Catalog for *Using Honey Bees to Pollinate Crops*:

```
         LC Control No.: agr68000286
       LCCN Permalink: http://lccn.loc.gov/agr68000286
               000 00868cam a2200253 450
               001 3119241
               005 19881221000000.0
               008 691216s1968 dcua 000 0 eng c
               035 __|9 (DLC)agr68000286
               906 __|a 7 |b cbc |c orignew |d u |e ncip |f 19 |g
                   y-gencatig
               010 __|a agr68000286
               040 __|a U.S. Nat'l Agr. Libr. |c DLC |d DLC
               050 10 |a S21 |b .A483 no. 549
               070 0_|a 1 Ag84L no. 549
               110 1_|a United States. |b Entomology Research Service.
               245 10 |a Using honey bees to pollinate crops.
               260 __|a [Washington, |b U.S. Govt. Print. Off., |c 1968]
               300 __|a 7 p. |b illus. |c 24 cm.
               490 1_|a United States. Dept. of Agriculture. |v Leaflet
                   no. 549
               650 _0 |a Honeybee.
               650 _0 |a Pollination by insects.
               650 _3 |a Fertilization of plants by insects.
               650 _3 |a Apis mellifera.
               830 _0 |a Leaflet (United States. Dept. of Agriculture); |v
                   no. 549.
```

Figure 5.2   Metadata in HTML

```
<HTML>

      <HEAD>

            <META NAME="DC.title" content="Honeybees
            Digital Collection">
            <META NAME="DC.description" content="Digital
            collection of materials related to
            honeybees. The collection was built by Prof.
            Joe Smith's BIO235 class. Maintainted by the
            Langstroth University Digital Repository
            Program.">
            <META NAME="DC.subject.keywords"
            content="digital library, European honey
            bees, Colony Collapse Disorder, CCD, apis
            mellifera, honey, pollen" />
            <META NAME="DC.creator" content="Langstroth
            Univeristy Library">
            <META NAME="DC.date.created"
            content="2010-02-14">
            <META NAME="DC.date.modified"
            content="2010-03-05" />
            <META NAME="DC.date.reviewed"
            content="2010-03-05">
            <META NAME="DC.language"content="eng">
            <META NAME="DC.format" content="html">

      </HEAD>

<BODY>
```

Figure 5.3   EXIF Metadata

Name	Size	Type	Date Modified	Date Picture Taken	Dimensions
IMG_0011.jpg	1,807 KB	JPG File	10/26/2008 9:23 AM	9/10/2008 7:09 PM	2448 x 3264
IMG_0012.jpg	1,788 KB	JPG File	10/26/2008 9:23 AM	9/10/2008 7:09 PM	2448 x 3264
IMG_0013.jpg	1,793 KB	JPG File	10/26/2008 9:23 AM	9/10/2008 7:10 PM	2448 x 3264
IMG_0014.jpg	1,965 KB	JPG File	10/26/2008 9:23 AM	9/10/2008 7:11 PM	3264 x 2448
IMG_0016.jpg	1,553 KB	JPG File	10/26/2008 9:23 AM	9/10/2008 7:11 PM	2448 x 3264
IMG_0017.jpg	1,551 KB	JPG File	10/26/2008 9:23 AM	9/10/2008 7:11 PM	2448 x 3264
IMG_0020.jpg	1,633 KB	JPG File	10/26/2008 9:23 AM	9/10/2008 7:17 PM	2448 x 3264
IMG_0021.jpg	1,615 KB	JPG File	10/26/2008 9:23 AM	9/10/2008 7:17 PM	2448 x 3264
IMG_0022.jpg	1,643 KB	JPG File	10/26/2008 9:23 AM	9/10/2008 7:18 PM	2448 x 3264
IMG_0023.jpg	1,754 KB	JPG File	10/26/2008 9:23 AM	9/10/2008 7:18 PM	2448 x 3264
IMG_0024.jpg	1,688 KB	JPG File	10/26/2008 9:23 AM	9/10/2008 7:18 PM	2448 x 3264
IMG_0025.jpg	1,674 KB	JPG File	10/26/2008 9:23 AM	9/10/2008 7:18 PM	2448 x 3264
IMG_0026.jpg	1,916 KB	JPG File	10/26/2008 9:23 AM	9/10/2008 7:19 PM	3264 x 2448

Figure 5.4   Metadata in word processing documents

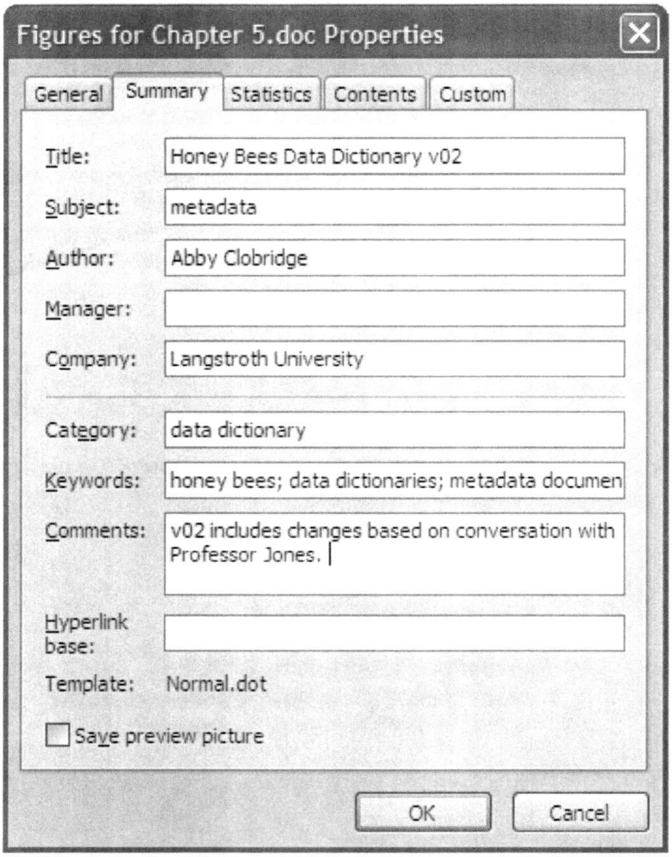

While both are conceptually similar, the day-to-day work tends to be vastly different. See Figure 5.5, 'Differences between traditional cataloging work and metadata work.'

Definitions

Controlled vocabulary: A limited set of defined terms that are allowed to be used in a field for a particular metadata schema.

Figure 5.5	Differences between traditional cataloging work and metadata work

- Work with multiple schemas.
- Data is not permanent.
- Work with multiple controlled vocabularies.
- Rarely use authority records.
- Minimal overlap between digital objects – most are unique.
- Heavier reliance on judgment when cataloging digital objects because of lack of definitive information, authority files.
- Pace – often have large quantities of objects to describe.
- Complexity of digital objects themselves – compound records, born digital objects. Books are easier to describe in terms of physical materials. Describe the object captured within the digital image plus the digital image. Example: for a photograph of a construction site: the digital photograph (who took the photo, what camera, file size, file format, date of the photograph, date of scan) plus the site represented in the photo (creator = architect, location of the site, purpose of the site, is the building part of a campus or larger complex?, dates of construction, dates of renovation).

Crosswalk: A document mapping the relationships between fields of different metadata schemas. Example: the Getty Crosswalk.[1]

Data dictionary: A formal document describing the metadata schema for a particular collection, defining each field, how data in each field is formatted, which controlled vocabularies are used, and all other pertinent structural and descriptive information about the metadata schema.

Dublin Core: the most widely used metadata schema within digital repositories. Also, the metadata structure used in harvesting.

Elements: Fields within a metadata schema.

Encoding: The process of tagging or marking up a file (usually one that is text based) using XML or another markup language to make the file facilitate computer processing. See Figure 5.6, 'Encoding' for example.

| **Figure 5.6** | Encoding

Title, author, publication date without encoding

Langstroth's Hive and the Honey-Bee: The Classic Beekeeper's Manual
L.L. Langstroth
1853

Title, author, publication date after encoding

<title>Langstroth's Hive and the Honey-Bee: The Classic Beekeeper's Manual</title>
<author>L.L. Langstroth</author>
<publication_date>1853</publication_date>

Folksonomies: User-created metadata tags for objects – example: tags applied to photographs in Flickr.

Granularity: High level of specificity when describing objects.

Harvesting: The process of copying metadata from objects in a collection and exporting the metadata to an external system.

OAI-PMH: Open Access Initiative Protocol for Metadata Harvesting.[2] The formal set of processes associated with harvesting.

Schema (or scheme): The structure of a set of elements within a given collection.

Standards: Metadata schemas adopted by national or international communities. Used to ensure consistency from one collection to another.

Thesaurus: A list of terms related to a particular subject or field of study. Terms are organized in such a way that their relationships to each are delineated or related terms are suggested. An example is the *Getty Art & Architecture Thesaurus.*[3]

Guiding principles

Some overarching principles to keep in mind when working with metadata:

Segment metadata production work.

- Break down tasks into the smallest possible pieces.
- Match the level of complexity of the tasks to the appropriate type of staff member.

Focus on progress over perfection.

- Don't get hung up on small details, especially at the expense of moving forward in a project.
- It's important to understand what can be easily edited later and what can't. Example: adding a new field versus adding more data to a field, cleanup of name authority records.

Use judgment to make decisions about quantity, usefulness, and necessity.

- It is not necessary to be exhaustive.
- Consider what information is useful or necessary and what is excessive. Adding unnecessary fields or details to metadata records is costly and harms usability.

Find a balance between the needs of the collection, the program, and standards.

Metadata work is fundamentally similar to traditional cataloging, but the day-to-day production work is vastly different and takes a different set of skills and expertise.

Types of metadata

Metadata can be broken into three main functions: description, administration, and structure. See Figure 5.7,

Figure 5.7   Types of metadata for digital repositories

> Description: information about the contents of the object; keywords or subject terms.
>
> Administration: information pertaining to rights and permissions, authorship, long-term preservation. Also includes technical details (file formats, software information) and use information (tracking how, when, and in what context an object has been used).
>
> Structure: information about compound objects – how parts of an object relate to each other. Examples: pages within chapters, chapters within books, the sequence in which images should be viewed.

'Types of metadata for digital repositories.' There is a nearly infinite amount of information that can be associated with a given digital object; the trick is to only collect, create, and store data that is of value. Ensuring that a particular field is closely tied to one of these three areas will help determine if that data is necessary.

Pay careful attention to administrative metadata. Just because you can capture information about a specific detail does not mean that you should. Think through the potential need for specific information. For example, most institutions creating digital collections do not need to indicate the scanner used to create a digital image in metadata associated with each item. It may not be relevant at all to capture that information, or it may suffice to indicate the scanners in a collection-level note.

Metadata standards and protocols

This section is intended to provide a very brief, practical overview to a few metadata standards and other key topics that it is necessary for those involved in metadata production to understand. More complex treatments of the subject are readily accessible, as are some excellent theoretical overviews. *Metadata fundamentals for all librarians* by Priscilla Caplan[4] provides an excellent, in-depth explanation of metadata for digital repositories, archival standards, and publishing. Consult Charles W. Bailey, Jr.'s *Institutional repository bibliography*, Chapter 7, 'Institutional Repository Metadata Issues,' for a list of articles and books on the subject.[5] *Cataloging & Classification Quarterly* published a special issue in 2009[6] about metadata and open access repositories. For current best practices in metadata production using Dublin Core, consult the CDP Metadata Working Group's 'Dublin Core Metadata Best Practices.'[7]

Dublin Core

Dublin Core[8] is the most pervasive metadata standard. It is general in nature and can be used to describe nearly any type of digital object because of its lack of specificity. Dublin Core comes in two varieties, unqualified (15 main elements) and qualified (an expanded set of elements, used to add more description to the 15 unqualified elements). See Figure 5.8, 'Dublin Core elements,' for a list of unqualified Dublin Core elements.

Unqualified Dublin Core is particularly important because it is the standard upon which OAI harvesting is built. Even if a collection does not use Dublin Core, a subset of the collection's fields need to be mapped to Dublin Core elements, so enough information must be conveyed in that small subset of fields to adequately describe objects in the collection.

The downside of Dublin Core is just this: because of its extremely general nature, it can be difficult to adequately describe the complexity of objects in the collection. In many cases, the workaround is to create a hybrid scheme – one

Figure 5.8 Dublin Core elements

The 15 elements comprising "simple" or unqualified Dublin Core:

Title	Contributor	Source
Creator	Date	Language
Subject	Type	Relation
Description	Format	Coverage
Publisher	Identifier	Rights

In Qualified Dublin Core, the 15 elements are still in place, although some elements have additional "qualifying" elements to refine their meaning or assign values to elements. In addition, a few new elements are included in Qualified Dublin Core. For example:

Element	Qualifiers
Date	Created
	Valid
	Available
	Issued
	Modified
	Date Accepted
	Date Submitted

The Dublin Core web site[1] includes the most up-to-date information about elements and qualifiers.

---

[1] *Dublin Core metadata initiative.* (n.d.). Retrieved January 30, 2010 from http://dublincore.org

that uses Dublin Core as its basis but uses additional fields to describe its nuances. However, if the collection will eventually be harvested, it is important that the fields that will be mapped to unqualified Dublin Core and that this configuration of data will be useful enough that the object can be retrieved and its description meaningful.

Dublin Core is also noteworthy because it is the standard that comes out of the box with several major repository systems including DSpace and CONTENTdm. In both of these systems, it is possible to add more fields, but Dublin Core is the starting point for metadata work.

VRA Core

For libraries working with collections of art (slide libraries, museums, art galleries), VRA Core[9] is another important standard to work with. VRA Core makes a distinction between a work (i.e., a work of art – the original object) and its surrogate (i.e., the digital image of the object). This distinction can help describe objects, especially artwork, as it is important to denote both sets of dates (when the work was created and when the photograph of the work was created), agents (i.e., creators – the work's artist and the photographer who was responsible for the photograph), etc.

VRA Core also has specific fields for information particularly important to works of art – the nationality or culture of an artist, the style or period in which an object was created, etc. While this level of detail is important to indicate for artwork, it will not be conveyed in the OAI harvested data.

Other metadata standards

Dublin Core and VRA Core are two of the most commonly used metadata standards in digital repositories at academic institutions. However, a number of other specialized standards exist and are more appropriate for individual collections. Be sure to investigate the range of standards before creating your own, and understand how the standards work together with other existing collections at your institution.

Some other metadata standards include:

- TEI (text-based documents such as manuscripts)
- METS and MODS (books, complex objects)
- PREMIS (preservation)
- FDGC (GIS data)
- PB Core (news/public broadcasting)
- IEEE LOM (learning objects)
- EAD (finding aids)
- Darwin Core (biology)
- ONIX (publishing).

When working with various standards, be sure to consult a crosswalk to understand the relationships between elements of different standards.

Homegrown or hybrid metadata schemas

Existing standards don't always meet the needs of every collection. Particularly for collections that are built to support specific curricular needs or administrative needs, it is quite likely that a ready-to-go standard will not be flexible enough to allow for the level of granularity needed to appropriately describe objects in that collection. In these cases, you will need to create your metadata schema or work with a few standards to create a hybrid that will serve the needs of your users.

For example, in the World War II Poster Project, a collection created by students in a history course, students wanted to include some additional fields such as the date of their course, their professor's name, and their own names. While this information will not be harvested, it was important for the students to include it in the collection in a marked-up, meaningful way rather than listing all of the data in subject fields.

A–Z of metadata work

Metadata responsibilities fall into a few different areas: some one-time decisions and intellectual work that need to occur at the start of a new project or collection, a significant amount of production-related work related to creating metadata for any group of digital objects, and long-term enhancements and authority control.

Selecting or defining a schema

At the start of a project, the metadata specialist needs to select a standard to follow, develop a new schema for that collection, or create a hybrid between an existing standard and a locally developed schema. This work is of critical importance and takes a high degree of planning and skill, and a deep understanding of how the collection will be used. See Figure 5.9, 'Questions to address in schema selection.'

Data dictionaries and crosswalks

After a scheme is determined, the metadata librarian responsible for the project should document the structure of the schema and define each element in the form of a data

Figure 5.9   Questions to address in schema selection

How will the collection be used? Are there connections between this collection and any other collections at the institution? Externally?
Is there an existing standard that will address all (or most) of the needs of this collection? If so, what standard? Do any fields need to be added?
What is the format for data in each field? Which fields use a controlled vocabulary? Is the controlled vocabulary from an existing thesaurus or do you need to define a set of terms?
Which fields will need to repeat? Which fields are tied to other fields (i.e., which fields are grouped together in one table)?
What are the overlaps between fields in this collection and in other collections at the institution? Is the proposed structure allowing for consistency between these points?
Is this collection going to be harvested? If so, it must be mapped to unqualified Dublin Core. Does the mapping make sense?

dictionary. The data dictionary should be clear enough that anyone involved in the project can understand what is required for each field and how its data should be formatted. Each field should be defined – what is its purpose? What is the source of its data? Is data using a controlled vocabulary? If so, what is the list of terms to use? Or do terms come from a specific thesaurus? Which one? See Figure 5.10, 'Structure of data dictionary,' and Figure 5.11, 'Sample data dictionary entry,' for details. The data dictionary for a project is a key living document. If changes are made during the course of a project, the data dictionary should be updated and re-distributed immediately.

In addition to writing the data dictionary, the metadata librarian should also map out how this schema will relate to other schemas used within the program. This exercise is helpful in seeing how data from different collections connects to each other and might illuminate points in which overlapping

Figure 5.10 Structure of data dictionary

Collection title
Author
Dates:

        Date of original publication
        Date of last revision

Table of contents, including list of each field

Explanatory text (if necessary)

For each field:

        Field Name
        Required Field? (Yes/No)
        Definition/Description
        Format
        Scope
        Rules
        Example

Figure 5.11 Sample data dictionary entry

Field name:	Title
Required:	Yes
Description:	A phrase used to identify the image.
Format:	Capitalize all words except articles, prepositions, and conjunctions. Do not use articles at the beginning of the title. Write out all abbreviations. Do not use a period at the end of the title.
Scope:	If a title must be synthesized from the record description, include only enough information to uniquely identify the object.
Rules:	Do not start a title with a number or year. Descriptive information should remain in the "Description" field.
Examples:	"Student Playing Tennis" "Gardner Hall and Olin Hall" "Portrait of Catherine K. Jones" "William C. Ellenton" "Women's 1985 Varsity Tennis Team" "Presidents William C. Ellenton and Charles H. Smith" "Map of Campus"

data is not structured in the same way but should be. For instance, if some collections have one field for 'Publication Information' but other collections are using separate fields for "Publisher", "Published Date," and "Publication Location," it might be wise to rethink the strategy.

In addition to reviewing internal crosswalks, a metadata librarian should also review crosswalks describing how standards connect to each other to be sure that the schema for this collection aligns with national and international standards. The Getty maintains a metadata standard crosswalk mapping the connection between several commonly used standards including Dublin Core, CDWA, EAD, and MARC, among others.[10]

Production

Once the collection structure has been defined, metadata will need to be produced for each object. There are a few ways to work with metadata, depending on the repository system. The simplest and most efficient way to work with metadata before objects have been uploaded into a repository is via a spreadsheet if the system will allow it. (Most systems have support for uploading a comma-delimited .txt file exported from a spreadsheet or an XML file.) Using spreadsheet software such as Microsoft Excel will allow for fast, easy processing of large quantities of records in one batch. If coordinated properly, different people can work on different fields at the same time and spreadsheets can be merged together before being uploaded.

Working on metadata in spreadsheets allows you to easily see inconsistencies in data captured on that particular spreadsheet, but it won't allow you to automatically compare data from that document with live data in your repository.

In other systems, records need to be worked on individually as part of the process to ingest a digital object and create a record for that object and its associated data. In this case, the entire record needs to be created at one time by one person. If your emphasis is on efficiency and working with minimal resources, it is highly recommended to try to upload data in batches.

Metadata production often requires a combination of work: creating metadata for certain fields from scratch; doing research for selected fields; and using notes on the back of photographs to piece together information.

To process existing metadata from outside sources (including vendors or faculty donating digital objects to the collection), most of the work will involve reformatting data, separating data from one field into several fields or vice versa, adding additional information to each record, or converting data from fields to controlled vocabularies. See Chapter 6, 'Collection building' for additional notes about working with content owners to facilitate metadata production.

Most of the time associated with metadata work happens at this point.

Cleanup and enhancements

One of the most difficult principles to embrace for those working in metadata – and yet one of the most essential principles if you are working with limited resources – is progress over perfection. By this, I mean that metadata does not need to be perfect and that on-going cleanup work and enhancements are part of the process. I would rather have live digital objects in a repository with metadata at approximately 75 percent completed or 'perfect,' than wait for that remaining 25 percent. Much of the detail work happens in the final 25 percent, and if someone is not driving the project forward, the collection can easily stall at that point. However, it is important to understand what data is essential to make the collection usable for its original purpose. If you can't find an object you need because its title is incorrect, the collection is not valuable. But if you are trying to add detailed, descriptive information about the symbolism of a bowl in a painting or you are adding subject-oriented keywords that are not explicitly necessary, it is more important to get the object into the live collection and add those keywords later.

The most convincing argument for the 75 percent rule is that the other 25 percent can be enhancements or cleanup after the collection is live. In some cases, it is easier to identify what fields need cleanup work after all of the objects have been uploaded, and it is easier to see inconsistencies from one collection to another.

Enhancing the metadata is different from cleaning up inconsistencies. As part of long-term curation, the metadata team can add additional subject terms from a locally developed taxonomy or industry thesaurus, incorporate user-created folksonomies and tags into records, and compare user searching behavior with record retrieval. What kinds of searches are users performing? And are they getting the results you would like for them to find? If not, what data can you add to records to facilitate this process?

Over time, users begin to search collections for different reasons than how the collections were originally conceived. This new interest in a collection may lead to metadata enhancements as well. See Chapter 10, 'Assessment' for details.

Collection-level work

After a collection is live, the focus shifts from getting objects and their metadata into the repository to facilitating use of the collection. Much of the work at this point is tied to marketing and outreach, but there are two areas in particular that are still within the domain of metadata: creating collection-level records for the integrated library system (ILS) and preparing collections for harvesting (if applicable).

Creating a collection-level record for the library's catalog is a straightforward process. For each collection, project, or group of objects that you would like to showcase, create a record in the library catalog. If your library makes records available to other institutions through systems such as OCLC's WorldCat, only export records for collections that are publicly accessible.

Harvesting

The last major step in metadata work is preparing it to be harvested as a means of more broadly disseminating the collection. Harvesting is the process in which metadata records are scraped from their original source and replicated in another collection – it is a mechanism to connect repositories to each other and repositories to aggregators. The digital objects themselves remain in their source collection, but a copy of the metadata record is then accessible through other aggregator systems and more easily exposed to search services.

The Open Access Initiative Protocol for Metadata Harvesting (OAI-PMH)[11] is the formal process by which harvesting occurs. OAI-PMH is a set of six steps or services to transfer metadata via XML through HTTP. These HTTP calls happen on a regular basis, allowing for ongoing data refreshes and additions to collections.

The other possibility for harvesting is for static repositories. Instead of building an OAI-compliant repository, the data owner does a one-time XML export of metadata and leaves the XML file on a web-accessible server. This is an easier process for repository owners, but involves more customization and manual work for the OAI aggregator repository. Many repository systems are set up to handle OAI-PMH and require minimal customization. If OAI-PMH is a possibility, it is the preferred mechanism for harvesting.

Non-standard schemas and harvesting

While there is value in describing various bits of information about an object, the smaller details may not be carried with the object's record outside of its native schema. However, the information may not be necessary – especially within the context for which the collection was created. It is important to understand how objects will be represented within various contexts and learn how to balance these sometimes competing needs.

Often, these issues are minor. For instance, many universities have art/art history collections that include large batches of images licensed from vendors. Faculty sponsors of such a collection might request that the metadata schema include a field to specify artists' gender to enable a typical student search such as: 'women artists of the 19th century.' Within Dublin Core, the only way to describe artists' gender would be through subject fields. However, this will not convey the difference between a work of art created *by* a woman and a work of art *about* or *depicting* a woman.

In this instance, adding a 'gender' field to the metadata schema causes few repercussions. While the field will not be included in an OAI harvest, the point is moot since the collection itself is not harvestable. This particular collection includes a number of images that were licensed from vendors. These licenses restrict access to the campus community.

While there are plenty of advantages to working strictly within a metadata standard, this example is designed to demonstrate that it is important to consider the primary purpose of a collection and how those users need to be able to find and use objects. It is more important to weigh potential benefits with negative repercussions when making decisions such as this. Sometimes the local needs outweigh the need to work with international standards, particularly if the purpose of the collection is to support an internal (curricular, administrative) need. If the focus of the collection is the public, the balance more easily shifts in favor of consistency and standards.

Tools to support metadata production

Once an institution has begun to develop consistent workflows, it is worth investing time to examine processes and available resources. Some questions to consider: are we consistently spending time to process batches of data in exactly the same way? If we had tools that were simple enough to use, could other people help with metadata production? If so, consider building tools to support your environment or adopting existing tools. For instance, build a series of metadata 'tools' such as Excel macros to speed up routine processes:

- capitalizing the first word in a given field;
- deleting articles at the start of a particular field;
- converting 'circa' dates to date ranges, converting centuries to date ranges;
- extracting commonly used words from a particular spreadsheet and assigning them as keywords;
- maintaining a list of keywords added to records and checking new keywords against a list.

All of these tasks can be set up within Excel as a macro and take far less time than manually running each process.

If you are looking for ways to bring in outside help to create metadata, generate tools in familiar software. For instance, the repository team at Bucknell University created a Microsoft Word template for creating new EAD-compliant finding aids. Special collections staff and student workers were able to work within this template. Commonly used EAD elements were each given a text-input field. Special collections staff could work on the finding aid over time rather than needing to submit all content at once via a web interface. Once the finding aid was complete, repository staff could encode the input text into XML with one click.

At Lafayette College, an institution with only one full-time staff member dedicated to supporting digital collection work, the repository team wanted to create a 'distributed' metadata production environment to get other individuals involved.[12] Users are given accounts and log into a web interface. From there, users input data into various forms and the repository's librarian exports data as CSV or TSV. Student workers can assist with metadata production as part of their scanning work, or other librarians can assist on specific projects. This tool – or a similar one – could greatly benefit many small repository teams by creating a much larger potential workforce to assist with metadata production.

None of these tools are particularly complex; tools do not need to be big, expensive, or complicated in order to work. Identify the tasks, consider the audience, and develop tools in response to those needs, ideally using interfaces or applications your potential workforce is already comfortable using. Make the barriers for adoption as low as possible, and don't overly complicate your objectives. Start with a proof-of-concept tool; test with the intended audience; and continue to adapt, build, or develop. Most importantly, keep it simple.

Complexity of metadata work

In sum, the complexity of metadata work stems from several factors:

- The standards themselves: the range of standards, limitations of standards, sheer number, and constant evolution.
- Lack of authority, sources for data.
- Quantity and pace. A collection can easily include several thousand items, many of which might not come to the library with any metadata.
- Creating records from scratch.
- Changes in user behavior, user expectations – tagging (Flickr) where users are expecting to find something. There is a big difference between users looking for something general and something specific.
- Balance between progress and perfection.
- Metadata work is never really finished. Enhancements can always be carried out later.
- Just because you can add a field or a bit of data doesn't mean you should. It can be difficult to know when to stop.
- Lack of subject-matter expertise can be challenging, frustrating, but also invigorating.

The hands-on metadata workshop

The only way to truly learn about metadata is to work with it. Create some sample collections using real digital objects from a personal collection or samples from a university's archives. Think about the different contexts in which the collection might be used. What would an ideal schema look like? Practice writing data dictionaries and crosswalks for collections. If you are in the job market, put some sample collections and the associated documentation together on a website. Access to a live repository system is not necessary to demonstrate an understanding of metadata.

Another option is to practice the tasks described in the metadata workshop outlined in Appendix 1, 'Introduction to Metadata workshop.' This workshop was designed to teach a group of traditional catalogers about metadata, but it has also been used to provide an overview of metadata production to groups of library and IT staff and a group of CIOs. It can easily be adapted to any target audience.

Conclusion

All work that goes into building a digital collection is important, but metadata is the single-most critical set of responsibilities – and often the most overlooked. Without useful data constructed in a meaningful way, objects will only be found if a user stumbles upon them. Metadata is the key to making objects findable, within the repository system and through external search engines. While the content owner or author originally thought of his or her object in one context, it is up to the metadata team to craft data in such a way that users can find and use the object for completely different purposes. Metadata work is time consuming. Much of the work in the early stages of building a collection requires a great deal of expertise; production work requires varying levels of expertise. Don't underestimate the amount of time metadata work will take on a given project.

Notes

1. Baca, M., Harpring P., Ward J., and Beecroft A (eds) (n.d.). *Metadata standards crosswalk*. Retrieved January 30, 2010 from http://www.getty.edu/research/conducting_research/standards/intrometadata/crosswalks.html

2. Open archives initiative (n.d.). Retrieved January 30, 2010 from http://www.openarchives.org

3. *Art & architecture thesaurus online* (n.d.). Retrieved January 30, 2010 from http://www.getty.edu/research/conducting_research/vocabularies/aat/

4. Caplan, P. (2003). *Metadata fundamentals for all librarians*. Chicago, IL: American Library Association.

5. Bailey, C.W. Jr. (2009) *Institutional repository bibliography*. Retrieved January 30, 2010 from http://www.digital-scholarship.org/irb/metadata.htm

6. Babinec, M. and Mercer, H. (2009). Introduction: Metadata and open access repositories. *Cataloging & Classification Quarterly*, 47(3), 209–211.

7. Dublin Core metadata best practices, version 2.1.1. (2006) Retrieved January 31, 2010 from http://www.bcr.org/dps/cdp/best/dublin-core-bp.pdf

8. Dublin Core metadata initiative (n.d.). Retrieved January 30, 2010 from http://dublincore.org

9. VRA Core (n.d.). Retrieved January 30, 2010 from http://vraweb.org/projects/vracore4/

10. Baca, M., Harpring P., Ward J., and Beecroft A. (eds) (n.d.). *Metadata standards crosswalk*. Retrieved January 30, 2010 from http://www.getty.edu/research/conducting_research/standards/intrometadata/crosswalks.html

11. Open archives initiative (n.d.). Retrieved January 30, 2010 from http://www.openarchives.org

12. Luhrs, E. (2008) *MetaDB: A distributed metadata creation tool*. Retrieved January 30, 2010 from http://www.departments.bucknell.edu/isr/DIG/MADLC/MADLC-EricLuhrs.pdf

6

Collection building: project proposals, planning, and implementation

Introduction

Building collections is at the heart of digital repository work for most practitioners. Identifying potential projects, making connections with content owners, building partnerships, working with objects, launching new projects, and continuing the long-term maintenance associated with collections are the bread and butter of repository work. Even so, it is important to have a good mastery of digitization techniques. The *BCR's CDP Digital Imaging Best Practices, Version 2.0*[1] is an excellent resource, particularly its sections on scanning, working with digital images, and quality control.

The focus of this chapter will be on:

- project proposals and the review process;
- project planning;
- tips and tricks to efficiently process quantities of digital objects;
- strategies for launching new collections.

While it can be tempting to just jump in and start scanning photographs or collecting digital objects, I highly recommend following a formal project management approach. Decisions should be made within the context of the digital program as a whole, not just at the project level. Working within a project management framework will help to keep all involved parties on the same page, and it will help guide the decision-making process.

Projects are a series of inter-related activities focused on a unique goal, occurring over a set period of time. There is a defined start and end to projects. Within the context of digital repositories, getting a digital collection built and launched (including post-launch discussions to evaluate processes) would be projects. Long-term operational work and maintenance of that collection would not be project work – it is handed over from the project team to the repository team.

Project management is a formal set of processes associated with projects. It usually includes several groups of processes:

- project initiation: proposals and the review process;
- planning;
- implementation;
- monitoring;
- closing (collection launch).

Details about each of these phases within the context of digital repository work will be discussed throughout this chapter.

Guiding principles

While most of the work is similar for anyone involved in digital repositories, this chapter will focus on aspects related to collection building through a programmatic approach and ways to keep collection building manageable with limited resources. Within this vein, guiding principles for collection building include:

- During the early stages of the repository program, start with small, manageable pilot projects. Use pilot projects as a learning experience for the staff and to establish and tweak processes. Tackle more ambitious projects after the team has successfully completed a few pilot projects.

- Use the repository steering group to make decisions about which projects to select for implementation. These decisions are potentially political in nature; take advantage of the steering group for these difficult decisions – they should not be the responsibility of one individual.

- Invest time in the proposal review process. Use the process as a way to get to know potential partners and gather information to wisely make decisions.

- Use a formal project management framework. Stick to it.

- Have potential collection sponsors submit formal project proposals.

- Think about the program as a whole when selecting projects. How do collections fit together? Is there a way to create a collection that accomplishes multiple objectives rather than creating several separate but overlapping collections?

During project implementation:

- Use technology to create efficient processes.

- Get creative in defining processes. Create workflows that meet the needs of your project team, particularly the needs of the content owner.

- Emphasize production over craft with the project team.

Project initiation: proposals and the review process

Project proposal

After the one-time work of creating a strategic plan for the repository program is completed, the main responsibilities of the digital repository steering group are related to initiating projects – specifically, determining which projects to implement. In order to facilitate this process, the digital repository steering group should codify project selection criteria, create a template for project proposals, support potential collection sponsors throughout the proposal process, and ultimately select projects to implement.

It is helpful to make a significant amount of information available to potential proposal authors so they fully understand the process for proposals and – more importantly – the processes and resources involved in building collections. Building a new collection is a significant investment of time and resources for both sets of partners as well as a commitment to long-term collection ownership and maintenance. It is imperative that this decision is not taken lightly and that proposers understand what will happen if their proposal is approved.

Be sure to make the following information available to potential proposers:

- criteria for project selection;
- members of the digital repository steering group (i.e., a list of who is reviewing proposals);
- stages of building a digital collection;
- proposal form.

All of this information can be posted on the repository program's website and should be updated as information changes.

Selection criteria should be straightforward and should match the mission and purpose of the digital program as described throughout the strategic plan. It should be concise and accessible to those considering writing proposals. Ideally, it should be posted on the program's website. Proposals can be accepted on an ongoing, rolling basis or libraries can put out an annual/semi-annual call for applications. Selection criteria should clearly reflect the mission and vision statements written during the strategic planning process.

Proposals themselves should echo the criteria selection and should include sufficient details so that the review committee is able to determine the approximate amount of time the library will need to invest in the project implementation, what resources are needed, what equipment will be used, and what the long-term implications are for digital storage and preservation. Proposals should address:

- Purpose: what is the purpose of this project? How will the collection be used?
- Collection: what is the source of materials for the collection? How many? In which format?
- Audience: who is the expected audience for this collection? Internal or external? Public or private?
- Partnership: what can the proposer contribute in terms of expertise, time, staff, and funding?

See Figure 6.1, 'Sample proposal template,' for an example.

The steering group should also decide in what format they would like to receive applications. Most commonly, groups request e-mailed documents or have proposers fill out an online form. Some groups require that proposers stick to a highly structured form, while others allow for more flexibility as long as the relevant information is conveyed. While online forms lend themselves to consistency from one application to another,

Figure 6.1   Sample proposal template

Please submit documentation for each project you are proposing by answering the questions listed below. Submit a separate proposal for each project. Proposals should be submitted electronically to the Digital Repository Steering Group at digrepos@langstroth.edu. You will be contacted by a member of the team to discuss the next steps.

Project background

- Describe the project/collection you would like to develop.
- For what type(s) of audience is the finished resource intended? (e.g. students in Economics 101, all microbiology students, the scholarly community, general interest, genealogists.) Would this collection be available outside of the university community?
- Is this project related to other projects or collections on campus, in the library, or elsewhere? If so, provide details.
- How would you gauge the success of this project/collection? Please describe all plans for assessment.

Goals

- Outline the general goals of this project and describe the overall importance of this project/collection to the university community.
- Would this project/collection be tied to any classes at the university? If so, list classes and explain how students and faculty would be involved in creating the project or using the finished resource.
- Would this project/collection be tied to scholarship being conducted at the university? If so, list information about projects and names of faculty involved.
- Is this project part of a collaborative effort with groups within or outside of the university? If so, provide context, contact information, and relevant details.
- Does this project have ties to the local community? If so, please explain.
- What is the timeframe in which you would hope to complete this project? Are there any anticipated constrictions on the timeframe such as a leave of absence that would affect the timeline of this project? If so, explain.

Materials

- Describe in as much detail as possible the materials to be included in the project. What is the physical format of the materials? What is the size of the collection? Describe in whatever terms make sense for these materials (Examples: 10 hours of footage on 50 mini DV tapes; 5,000 slides; 1,000 photographs.)

- What is the physical condition of the materials? Are there preservation issues that need to be addressed? Address issues such as fragility of resources, damaged condition, fading colors.
- Please describe the copyright status as you best understand it to be for the involved materials.
- Are you the owner of these materials? If not, who is?
- Is the owner of the material willing to consider having it sent to a commercial vendor if this is determined to be the best approach for digitization? If not, why?

Additional information

- Please provide any additional information that might help us better understand your proposed project.

---

they can be time consuming to change or edit. More importantly, proposal authors need to fill out the form in one session. Having authors submit their own documents ideally encourages proposal authors to invest more thought into the process.

A word of caution: if a faculty member or administrator is interested in pursuing a project but does not want to submit a formal proposal, it is a good indication of things to come. If possible, do not proceed with this project. Projects undertaken as partnerships require that both sides of the partnership contribute something – time, energy, effort, resources. If the potential partner does not want to submit a written proposal, it is usually an indicator that this person will be challenging to work with on the project itself. For a further discussion on ideal partners, see Chapter 7, 'Content recruitment and marketing.'

The review (and negotiation) process

Members of the digital repository steering group should review proposals, discuss how the project fits into the mission and scope of the digital repository program, the general feasibility of the proposal, whether the resources to complete the project are available, the potential partnership between the individual or department requesting the proposal and the repository staff, the importance of the project, and long-term commitment by the library/repository team.

Many proposals will need additional follow-up – either in the form of a discussion between the project sponsor and members of the steering group or as a feasibility study, conducted by repository team members. Proposal authors often do not convey enough detail in their proposals to allow the repository team to get a full understanding of the potential issues surrounding projects. It is better to invest additional time to set up a follow-up meeting and be sure that all questions are addressed rather than deal with surprises in the course of a project.

Collection size

Pay careful attention to the objects themselves. Proposal authors often originally want all of their objects to be included in a collection, but particularly for collections of digital images, it is unnecessary and expensive to do so. While there might be some minor distinctions between several nearly identical images, it might be useful to 'weed' the collection to a more manageable size. Every object that gets ingested into a repository costs the university money. Not only does the object need to be identified, processed, ingested and have metadata created for it, but also there are long-term costs associated with storing and maintaining the objects. From a usability perspective, it can be overwhelming for users to get too many nearly identical results, making it difficult for them to find exactly what it is that they were looking for.

If the proposer is not amenable to these changes, try to negotiate a phased approach to the project launch. In phase one, launch with a subset of the full collection. After the collection is launched, plan to revisit this discussion and move forward with a second phase, including another large batch of images. Often, by the time the first phase is launched, the content owner does not feel so strongly about including additional images. Alternatively, it can be clear at that point that you do in fact need to include all of the objects in the collection. These collection development issues can be easily addressed as part of the review process, but it becomes more challenging to deal with them after a green light has been given to move forward.

Collection structure and access issues

Often, authors of proposals request that their collections are private or access is restricted to students enrolled in their courses or to colleagues they are working with on projects. Frequently, content owners think that the collections are not relevant to other individuals, therefore they should not be made publicly available. This mindset is slowly changing with the Web 2.0 world as sites such as Flickr and YouTube are becoming more common and more heavily populated.

Because of the investment of resources necessary to build any collection, it is fiscally responsible for repository programs to encourage content owners to make their collections as widely available as possible. Often, collections are used for entirely different purposes than how the content owner originally envisioned – with interesting, creative results. For example, a collection of archival historical photographs of a university is used by a group of students for their senior engineering project.

Fortunately, with most systems, there are options besides publicly accessible and completely restricted. A middle ground that often appeals to content owners is to restrict access to the collection to the campus community – either people with a campus ID or anyone on campus, with access being restricted to those within the college's IP range.

Even so, it is up to those responsible for the digital repository program to decide what levels of access restriction the program will support. Many programs only support collections that are indeed publicly accessible, with a few exceptions due to licensing issues, privacy issues, or business needs. Many institutions have licensed digital images from vendors; these objects must be accessible only by members of the campus community.

Administrative departments often have other reasons for wanting to restrict access. Athletics departments may have licensing issues as well, and public relations departments may not want their images widely disseminated while they are actively using those images for magazines, brochures, and on the university's website.

In any case, be prepared to discuss these issues with proposers, and if your program is not going to support highly restricted personal collections, be sure that the strategic plan and program's mission statement reflect this decision. It might be necessary to defend this decision.

Legal issues

Digital collections inherently raise a number of legal issues: copyright, authors' rights, and privacy. Often, a conversation with a lawyer from the university counsel's office will settle any outstanding issues, but if the legal issues pose insurmountable (or excessively costly) challenges, the proposal cannot move forward.

Copyright is the most typical issue within digital repositories. Who owns the copyright for the objects intended to be included in the collection? If the objects are not original, someone else likely owns their copyright. Works of art have an additional level of complexity. Even if the works themselves are old enough that they should be in the public domain, museums may own licensing rights for all images of the works of art. For further details about the range of copyright issues or for resources to help determine copyright status of objects, consult the University of Texas Copyright Crash Course[2] or the Stanford University Libraries' Copyright and Fair Use website.[3]

At some schools, students sign a document when they arrive at the university that gives the institution permission to use photographs taken of them, thus providing a model release.

Other privacy-related issues may arise, depending on the nature of the digital objects. If students or faculty are interviewing people not affiliated with the university as part of their research, they should already be abiding by rules covered by institutional review boards or other nationally mandated regulations. However, it should be clear in any documentation signed by research study participants that their interviews will be collected and preserved in a digital repository and whether these interviews will be publicly accessible, restricted to the campus community, restricted to a group of researchers, in a dark archive, etc.

Each collection should include a signed intellectual property rights statement indicating that the copyright owner is granting non-exclusive rights to the library to include these objects in the digital repository. The statement should also indicate ownership of the objects.

Who owns the copyright for objects within a collection must be clearly documented. As part of the process to transfer digital objects, have content owners sign a statement indicating that they own the rights to deposit these items into the repository. Many content owners wish to retain copyright over their objects, in which case they are giving permission to the repository team to deposit their items, but they are not transferring copyright.

The repository team may wish to consider encouraging content owners to use a Creative Commons license.[4] Creative Commons has created several different licenses, each reflecting a different set of conditions upon which content owners can apply to their work. See Figure 6.2, 'Creative Commons licenses,' for information about licenses for the United States. Creative Commons licenses are available for many countries; be sure to use the correct license.

For repositories of scholarship, each individual contributor will need to sign a non-exclusive rights statement. Institutions have varying comfort levels with collecting and storing non-exclusive licenses. The steering group (including senior-level library administrators, if they are not part of the steering group) should discuss the issues around these statements: if such statements need to be signed, if a paper copy needs to exist or if a digital copy will suffice, who is responsible for keeping these documents, etc. Some institutions require a signed hard copy while others are comfortable with the owner's signature on an electronic document.

Many institutions are shifting to electronic check boxes much like end-user agreements on software, although not all are comfortable with this approach. The repository system DSpace includes such a step in the upload process. While this saves paperwork and avoids long-term issues of collecting and storing files, there are some potential problems with this approach. Most institutions do not require self-submission of objects; objects tend to be uploaded by a member of the library staff or a faculty member's assistant. The very nature

Figure 6.2	Creative Commons licenses[1]
Attribution *cc by*	This license lets others distribute, remix, tweak, and build upon your work, even commercially, as long as they credit you for the original creation. This is the most accommodating of licenses offered, in terms of what others can do with your works licensed under Attribution.
Attribution Share Alike *cc by-sa*	This license lets others remix, tweak, and build upon your work even for commercial reasons, as long as they credit you and license their new creations under the identical terms. This license is often compared to open source software licenses. All new works based on yours will carry the same license, so any derivatives will also allow commercial use.
Attribution No Derivatives *cc by-nd*	This license allows for redistribution, commercial and non-commercial, as long as it is passed along unchanged and in whole, with credit to you.
Attribution Non-Commercial *cc by-nc*	This license lets others remix, tweak, and build upon your work non-commercially, and although their new works must also acknowledge you and be non-commercial, they don't have to license their derivative works on the same terms.
Attribution Non-Commercial Share Alike *cc by-nc-sa*	This license lets others remix, tweak, and build upon your work non-commercially, as long as they credit you and license their new creations under the identical terms. Others can download and redistribute your work just like the by-nc-nd license, but they can also translate, make remixes, and produce new stories based on your work. All new work based on yours will carry the same license, so any derivatives will also be non-commercial in nature.

(Continued)

---

[1] Creative Commons (n.d.). *Licenses*. Retrieved January 25, 2010 from http://creativecommons.org/about/licenses

Figure 6.2	Creative Commons licenses (*cont.*)
Attribution *Non-Commercial* *No Derivatives* *cc by-nc-nd*	This license is the most restrictive of our six main licenses, allowing redistribution. This license is often called the "free advertising" license because it allows others to download your works and share them with others as long as they mention you and link back to you, but they can't change them in any way or use them commercially.

of the agreement is dependent upon the copyright owner indicating agreement, not the signature of a proxy.

Non-exclusive licenses include several key elements:

- a statement defining non-exclusive rights;

- permission to reformat the object in the future;

- permission to create 'clip' or 'highlight' packages for video;

- permission to write abstracts;

- permission to add and edit metadata.

Don't start from scratch when drafting a non-exclusive license. Search for examples of current such licenses from other institutions within your country to use as a starting point.

Steering group recommendations

Once you have reviewed a proposal, discussed any questions with the proposer, and solved any legal issues, the steering group should make a decision about whether or not to move forward with the project.

Possible recommendations by the steering group:

- Proposal accepted as is, pending final review.

- Proposal is accepted, pending changes indicated by the steering group and final review – for example, instead of including all 3,000 images in a collection, narrow down the set of images and focus on a much smaller subset.

- Proposal tentatively accepted, pending additional considerations (additional funding from within the university; additional resource allocation, etc) and final review.
- Suggest significant changes to the proposal and schedule further discussions to negotiate details.
- Apply for external funding – possibly with the library as a co-principal investigator on the grant application.
- Proposal is not feasible due to issues such as copyright, staffing, timelines, equipment, storage, etc.

As part of the review process, a tentative timeline will be established or, for a repository program with a large number of accepted proposals, the proposal should be tentatively assigned a spot in the queue.

Final review: the 10,000-foot view

After the steering group blesses a project, a project manager should be assigned to the project to work out final details and help shepherd the project as it moves to project planning and implementation. These details should be negotiated before the final green light has been given since this is the final go or no go point of the proposal review process.

If the project manager had not been part of the review process, this final review will give him or her an opportunity to familiarize him/herself with the proposal and collection and raise any additional issues that are found. From this point forward, the project manager should be the one to negotiate directly with the proposer rather than going through the steering group.

The final step in the review is to create a draft timeline and workflow. It is imperative that you go through one last reality check: confirm weeks/months when work will occur, what each member's responsibilities will be, and if additional resources have been promised to this project, finalize any details about that.

Project planning

After the final review occurs and the project has been given a go-ahead status, the project officially moves from the proposal stage to the planning stage. The project manager facilitates the work from this point forward.

Responsibilities for the project manager

The project manager (PM) is usually responsible for organizing the project, processes, workflow, budget, deadlines, and delegating tasks. A project manager is the general contractor of building digital collections. He or she oversees the entire project, communicates with external constituencies, handles the budget, and hires and manages skilled and unskilled labor. Essentially, the project manager ensures that a project moves forward on time, within budget, and accomplishes its goals and objectives. Project management work is extremely detail-oriented and requires an individual who can successfully (and comfortably) juggle multiple tasks, prioritize, and make decisions.

Some tasks that are the project manager's responsibility include:

- Organizing workflows, assigning work to staff.
- Adopting a metadata schema and overseeing metadata production. (Ideally, metadata work is delegated to the librarian responsible for metadata if such a librarian is available. If not, the PM is responsible.)

- Reformatting: determining specifications for digitization and whether digitization is being handled in house or outsourced.

- Managing the budget.

- Overseeing equipment procurement.

- Ensuring quality control and quality assurance for digital object processing and metadata production.

- Coordinating plans for storage and long-term maintenance of collection.

- Communication strategy for launch: writing articles, distributing press releases, posting announcements to listservs.

- Scheduling end-user training.

Many of these tasks should be handled by other members of the project team, but it is the PM's job to assign this work and ultimately take responsibility for it.

Setting up the work breakdown structure (WBS) is at the heart of this process. In short, the WBS is a chart of tasks, individuals, and deadlines. See Figure 6.3, 'Work breakdown structure chart,' for an example.

Figure 6.3   **Work breakdown structure chart**

Work category	Task	Who	Deadline
Images	Convert Autocad files to TIFFs	Jack	October 1
Metadata	Determine metadata schema	Sarah H.	October 1
Metadata	Write data dictionary	Sarah H.	October 15
Images	Scan photos from Professor Jones	Jack	October 20
Images	Quality control for images	Sean	November 10

The project manager is also responsible for setting milestones for the project – for example, finishing the preliminary metadata work (determining the schema, writing the data dictionary) or completing all digitization and image cleanup work. It is important for team morale, especially on longer projects, to acknowledge and celebrate milestones as you complete them.

Project management software

There are many different options for project management software applications. Many are free; several are open source; some require software installations, others are web-based applications. It can be helpful to use project management software to maintain the work breakdown structure, tie milestones to calendars, create a hierarchical list of tasks, view information in various reports and formats, or print lists of all of the assigned tasks for one person. Wikipedia maintains a current list of project management software to compare different applications.[5]

Most project management software packages include the ability to create a Gantt chart, a type of bar chart that shows project tasks in correlation to their schedule and it indicates how tasks are dependent upon each other. Gantt charts also indicate how far along in a given tasks you should be based on the timeline – i.e., today is March 23 which falls into project week four. These are the activities that should be underway, these activities should be finished, and these activities are left. See Figure 6.4, 'Gantt chart,' for an example.

Depending on your needs, using a spreadsheet might be a simpler way to maintain this information, although you will lose some of the functionality of specialized software such as being able to automatically create Gantt charts. If you are new to project management or you are managing a

Figure 6.4   Gantt chart

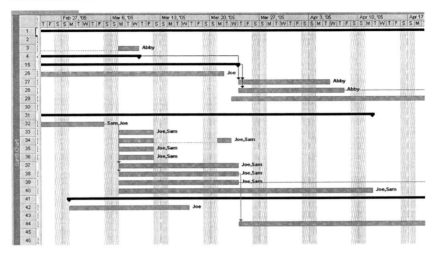

very large, very complex project with many people involved, it would be worth investing time in using specialized project management software so you can run the reports. After you have reached a comfort level with project management, the additional reports might not be necessary, although they are helpful if you are working with large teams.

Metadata work

During the project planning phase, the person responsible for metadata for this project will need to familiarize himself with the objects, the intended purpose of the collection, and any conversations related to metadata that occurred during the proposal review process. The main work related to metadata during the project planning phase is:

- Schema structure – use an existing standard, use an existing schema in use elsewhere at the institution, create a new schema, or create a hybrid between a few existing schemas.

129

- Write a data dictionary for the collection.
- Decide who will be responsible for content in each field.

See Chapter 5, 'Metadata' for a more complete discussion of the metadata work associated with preparing to build a collection.

After the schema has been defined, it is important to define the specifics of how data will be created for each field. What is the source of the data? Who will be responsible for each field? Will the content owner or someone he/she has delegated be involved in creating data for any fields? If so, how will that occur?

Project implementation

Assembling the collection

At the point where the project moves from planning to implementation, you need to start assembling all of the objects that will be included in the collection. For physical objects, identify where they are and if possible, move them to the space where production will occur. If physical objects are located in the archive or in a special collections department, work with the curator or archivist to develop a plan to transport the objects in and out of their space. Will the objects be moved all at once and for the duration of the project? Or will the objects be moved in batches? If it is the latter, develop a system to keep track of what objects (or folders or boxes) will be out of the archive at any given point in time. A simple clipboard might be sufficient, but it is important to keep track of where items are at any point in time and who is responsible for that particular batch of items.

Digital objects often come to the repository team in a disorganized fashion and may take a significant amount of work to organize. Content owners create their own mechanisms for organizing objects (particularly images). If the collecting has been occurring over a period of time, the organizational structure often breaks down, resulting in a mess of items in folders with names such as: 'New Folder,' '2009,' '2009 – New,' 'Junk,' etc. See Figure 6.5, 'Mindmap' for an example. Potentially useful metadata is often associated with folder structure and directory names, so be careful separating items from their folders until you have captured the metadata in some way. For instance, if working with

Figure 6.5 Mindmap[1]

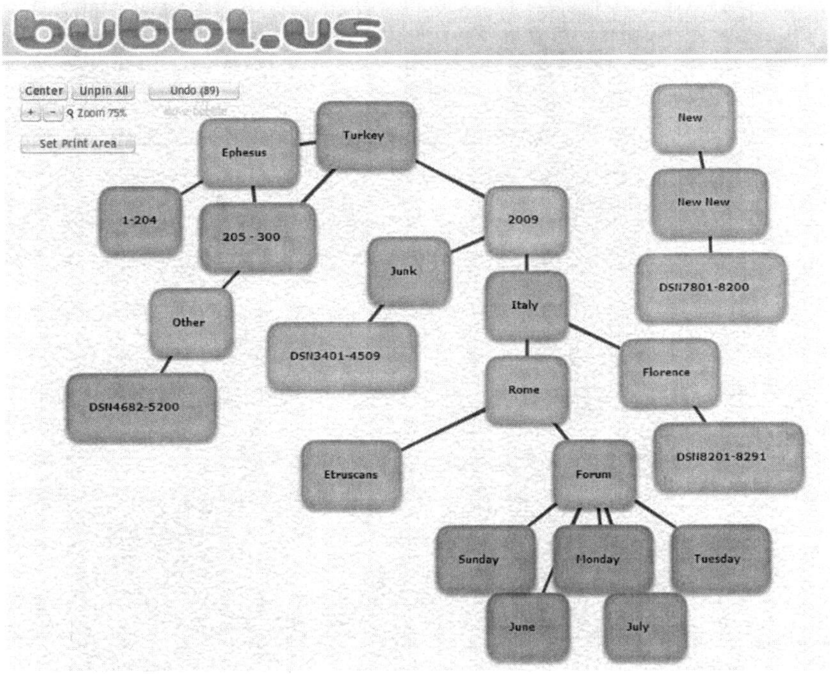

_____

[1] *Mindmap* (n.d.) Retrieved January 30, 2010 from http://www.bubbl.us

metadata associated with travel, images might be organized in hierarchical folders similar to this structure:

2009 → Italy → Rome → Vatican
2009 → Italy → Rome → Forum
2009 → Italy → Florence

Use clues such as folder structure to organize the contents and start creating metadata. Also use any other clues that might exist such as an itinerary from a trip. If the photographer set the date on his camera, you might be able to piece together information that could potentially be helpful.

Weeding

If you are planning to weed any content out of the collection, this is the appropriate time to do so – after the collection has been organized but before digitization starts for analog objects, and before metadata production begins in earnest. You do not want to invest staff time in costly metadata work and reformatting for objects that will not ultimately go into the collection. Work directly with the content owner on weeding.

Setting up a production environment

Library staff members sometimes have a difficult time making the transition to working in a production-type environment. The same is true for content owners, particularly faculty members, who are unaccustomed to working in this type of environment. Working with large quantities of data or objects requires a mental shift from thinking about the work being performed as *craft* to that of *mass production*. It is important for team members to make this mental change in how they think about their work; otherwise they can easily get distracted by focusing on perfecting one small detail or object.

Student employees, on the other hand, tend to work well in a production environment. They do not have any sentimental attachment to the objects themselves, and they typically work short shifts. Their focus is on their coursework and co-curricular activities, so work often is the part of the day when they 'zone out.' Production work is ideal for them as they can quickly accomplish repetitive tasks for large quantities of objects such as scanning, cropping, or cleaning images.

For a cost-effective workflow, tasks should be delegated so that the most appropriate person or group is responsible for a given task. Ideally, the most unskilled work should be assigned to the most unskilled laborers. If scanning a 4×6" photograph at 300 ppi takes two minutes per object and the collection includes 300 objects, scanning alone will take approximately 600 minutes. Hypothetically, a student costs $12/hour and a low-level staff member costs $20/hour.

600 minutes/60 minutes (1 hour) = 10 hours of work
10 hours × $12/hr. = $120
10 hours × $20/hr. = $200

In this example, the dollar amount is relatively close together, but this is an ideal scenario. Most of the objects that need to be scanned are oversized or inconsistent sizes, which significantly adds to the time. Also, because of the length of student employees' shifts, it is likely that a few different students over a few days would be responsible for that work, whereas one staff member would likely handle the entire workload. If this is true, the students will likely be more efficient and it will take them several hours less. The staff time would probably increase to at least 12 hours.

The bottom line: since this work is relatively unskilled in nature, assign it to your cheapest labor source. And if there is funding, consider outsourcing this task. Your staff can focus on other work; usually, outsourcing scanning is the more cost effective choice.

Batch processes

A hallmark of the production environment is using batch processes whenever possible. Separate tasks into discrete elements that can be done routinely, following a set of rules. Learn how to use your hardware and software's batch processing capabilities.

Many scanners include the ability to handle batch processes to scan either multiple images on a flatbed at the same time or a set of slides. If you are purchasing new scanning equipment, be sure to select one that can handle batches. Most mid-market scanners come with this capability, but check the model specifications before you make a purchase.

Items should be scanned in batches based on their size. Many scanning best practices recommend that you scan master files so the digital images are 3000 pixels on the longest side. To facilitate scanning, if you are working with large batches of images that are not all the same size, organize photographs into batches of similar/same shapes and sizes. Then indicate all pertinent information so student workers or staff are ready to scan, complete with instruction on what resolution to use, where to save scanned images, and filenames. If you use a worksheet for each folder or batch, employees can indicate who scanned those images and the date. Folders can then proceed down the assembly line for metadata and quality control. See Figure 6.6, 'Scan sheet,' to see an example.

Figure 6.6 Scan sheet

Scan sheet: Honeybee Project

Folder: bees_scotland   Folder ID: bees_scotland_001

Number of Images: 20

Image Details, Descriptions, Source Notes:

Photo number bees-scotland-005 is extremely fragile.

Scanning File Info/Notes:

   Scan at 300 ppi

   Filenames: bees_scotland_001.tiff to bees_scotland_020.tiff

Scanned by: Date:	Andrew September 8
Image QC: Date:	Joe September 20
Metadata by: Date:	Ellen October 5
Metadata QC: Date:	Susan October 10
Uploaded by: Date:	Joe October 15

Metadata production

For images, working with printouts in binders can be a useful way to manage the process. Consider giving your content owners a binder with printouts of their images and each image's filename. For some collections, a full-page printout of image thumbnails with their filenames works well. For other collections, larger versions of each image are necessary in order to indicate details.

Once you've given the content owner the binder, they can use it for several purposes: identifying which images to include in the collection and which can be skipped or deleted; creating a title or description for each image; or identifying details within each image. You can set up a spreadsheet for the content owner to use or, if he or she is not comfortable working in spreadsheet software, he/she can create a list in word processing software. If all else fails, the photos can be annotated directly on the printouts.

Excel tips and tricks

Mastering some tricks using Excel and batch processes in DOS will help automate some tasks that are used on a regular basis. See Figures 6.7 to 6.10 for some suggested processes to learn.

Monitoring

Throughout the project implementation, the project manager needs to routinely monitor the project. How are processes working? Do any changes need to be made to processes, work

Figure 6.7   Creating a text list of file names

Purpose: How to create a list of names of files (such as digital images) within a single directory that can be imported into Excel. PC Only.

From a PC: Start > Run.
Open: cmd
In DOS, navigate to the folder of images.
At DOS prompt:
dir /b c:\temp\data1.txt

Figure 6.8   Import list of file names into Excel

Purpose: Import a list of file names (or file names plus additional metadata) into Excel. PC Only.

> Open Excel.
> Data > Import External Data
> Navigate to .txt file created in above step.
> Text Import Wizard: Delimited
> Filenames will appear in column.

To capture other data associated with each file such as date of creation, repeat original process except at DOS prompt:

> dir > c:\temp\data2.txt

Figure 6.9   Alphanumeric formatting in Excel

Purpose: to create an alphanumeric incremental list of unique identifiers such as bees0001, bees0002, bees0003, etc.

From within Excel:

- Select column.
- Right click > Format cells
- Under the "Number" tab, select "Custom" as the Category type.
- In the area for "Type":
- "bees"0000
- Use quotes around any text
- Include one zero for each placeholder
- Cells will function as numbers.
- Enter "1"→ "bees0001"
- In next cell, type:
- =B1+1
- Value will change to: bees0002
- Select B2, drag down.

assignments, or timelines? Monitoring should not happen at the end of the phase but rather throughout. Weekly meetings with the project team are a good opportunity to check in with staff. The project manager should communicate often with the team and make project plans (including the work

---

Figure 6.10   Rename a batch of files using Excel and DOS

Renaming files

- In Excel: Repeat process.
- Change format to: "bees"0000".JPG"
- Fill down.
- Copy column.
- Open Notepad. Paste into Notepad.
- Copy from Notepad. Paste back into Excel. (Changes from formatting to text.)
- In next column:
- ="rename "&A1&" "&C1&" "
- Fill down.
- In next column:
- ="rename "&A1&" "&C1&" "
- Fill down.
- Copy column in Excel.
- Paste into Notepad.
- Save as .bat – Ex: rename_bees.bat
- In DOS, navigate to folder containing images.
- At prompt:
- C:\folder> c:\temp\rename_bees.bat

---

breakdown structure, calendars, and Gantt charts) available to the team. Team members usually appreciate having the opportunity to see how their tasks and responsibilities fit into the bigger picture. If someone is not on schedule to complete a task on time, the project manager can easily demonstrate how this will affect other team members and other activities that are relying on that task being completed.

Closing: launch

The last phase of project implementation is actually launching the collection. Besides making the collection live on a server, the project manager needs to do some outreach work. The steering group for the repository program should create a list of standard steps to take as part of a collection launch. See Chapter 7, 'Content recruitment' for a detailed list of outreach ideas.

Post-launch

Assessment

Even though project teams are expected to communicate issues with the project manager as issues arise, it is still important to take a step back after the project has been launched and talk about how the implementation went. What worked well? What didn't? What should be emulated again in the future? Were any processes that were used new? If so, how did they go?

A similar conversation should be had with the content owner to get his feedback. Notes from both sets of conversations should be included as part of the written documentation for this project.

Documentation

One of the last responsibilities for a project manager is to gather up relevant documents and write a report about the project. This report will serve as the final document detailing the collection's history. See Figure 6.11 for an outline of what to include in a collection report.

Ongoing work

While the project phase is completed after the collection has been launched, the repository team will still need to maintain the collection. The project manager should hand over the collection at this point to a repository curator who will then

Figure 6.11 Outline for collection report

> About the project team: list of members, content owner.
>
> About the collection: what type of objects, how many ingested by launch date.
>
> Project timeframe and plan: project timelines (anticipated and actual), Gantt chart, work breakdown structure, any other relevant reports.
>
> Metadata: the data dictionary, metadata schema.
>
> Outreach: what steps were taken to showcase this collection? What articles and press releases were written? Where were they distributed?
>
> Lessons learned: notes from the project wrap-up discussions, suggestions for the future.
>
> Assessment: how will this collection be evaluated? What intervals?
>
> Plans for the future

take over responsibilities. Long-term work includes digital preservation, adding to the collection, long-term metadata enhancements, reviewing log analyses, and any other work on the collection that occurs in the future.

Notes

1. *BCR's CDP Digital Imaging Best Practices Version 2.0* (2008). Retrieved January 31, 2010 from http://www.bcr.org/dps/cdp/best/digital-imaging-bp.pdf
2. Harper, G. (n.d.) *University of Texas Copyright Crash Course.* Retrieved January 31, 2010 from http://www.utsystem.edu/ogc/intellectualproperty/cprtindx.htm
3. Stanford University Libraries (n.d.) *Copyright and Fair Use.* Retrieved January 30, 2010 from http://fairuse.stanford.edu/
4. Creative Commons (n.d.). *Licenses.* Retrieved January 25, 2010 from http://creativecommons.org/about/licenses
5. Wikipedia (n.d). *Comparison of project management software.* Retrieved January 25, 2010 from http://en.wikipedia.org/wiki/Comparison_of_project_management_software

7

Content recruitment and marketing

Introduction

Content is the heart and soul of any repository program. Without interesting, carefully curated collections, the repository program's success will be limited. Fortunately, all institutions have access to a seemingly unlimited mass of potential content. It is the role of the repository steering committee and the repository coordinator to seek out potential content owners and build relationships with partners.

Guiding principles

Some principles to keep in mind as you solicit potential collections:

Don't make it about the library.
While it is a library-run program and service, it is designed to support the institution as a whole. Make that clear to content owners. The program is designed to showcase and disseminate their materials. While the library likely has great sources of content, if the first projects built are library-owned collections, it will be more challenging to recruit content

from external sources. Hold off on depositing much of the library's content until reaching critical mass.

Pick partners strategically.
Particularly when dealing with faculty, not all potential partners are created equally. Look for faculty members who are committed to the project, who have time to donate. Emphasize the collaborative nature of partnerships. Building a digital collection should not lead to a servitude environment; it should be a true collaboration between colleagues, each offering a different set of expertise.

If you build it, will they come? No. But if they build it, they will use it.
Get collection owners and partners involved in the collection-building process. The more invested content owners/sponsors are in the collection, the more apt they will be to use it.

Get creative.
Create collections around a theme, a current or upcoming event, or an historical event. Look for partners in unusual places.

Working with faculty

DRP seeks AEF: the Digital Repository Program seeks able and eager faculty

Working with the right partners can be one of the most rewarding parts of digital repository work. For the right faculty members, building a digital collection can support their research efforts, allow them to analyze information in a new way, or help solve teaching issues. But if done properly, most digital projects require a significant investment of a faculty member's time, so it is important that you work with individuals who have the potential to be good partners. The process is much like dating. Think about some of the ideal qualities you're looking for in a potential partner:

- high level of commitment;
- time availability;
- organization;
- flexibility;
- general understanding of copyright issues;
- willingness to play by the rules;
- willingness to collaborate, work as a partner.

You are also going to need to find someone whom you trust (and who trusts you), is easy to get along with, and does not have a fear of technology. One faculty partner (Russ Dennis, Associate Professor of Education, Bucknell University) once said after building a new digital collection, 'you can teach an old dog new tricks if you have a good enough teacher.' Faculty partners don't need to be particularly tech-savvy, but they do need to be willing to learn new skills – and learn from a librarian.

Piquing (and sustaining) interest among potential partners

Digital repositories lend themselves particularly well to visual displays and demonstrations. Take advantage of existing opportunities to meet and greet faculty or host your own. Set up a table or booth at new faculty orientation events. If possible, connect a laptop to a large high-definition monitor in the room to project a slideshow of images from collections.

Use additional laptops to give demonstrations to individuals who are interested in possibly building a collection or using objects from within existing collections.

Come to these events prepared with posters, slide show presentations, handouts, listserv signups, printouts of upcoming events, and business cards. Have generic business cards made for the repository program. Do not include names of individuals, but do include the URL for the repository's website.

If each collection has a small marketing budget associated with it, print business cards or postcards for each collection. Highlight some digital objects, and include a brief description of the collection, its owner, and how to access the collection. These cards can be used for so many purposes and can be printed at a bulk discount. If a project only has $100–$200 to spend on marketing materials, printing cards is the best investment. Take advantage of the visual nature of digital repository projects, and be sure to include diverse and interesting images from the collection on the cards.

Once you make connections at these events, follow-up with faculty. Have a sign-up for faculty to register for an online newsletter or mailing list, but don't be pushy. Entice faculty to attend upcoming events such as a digital image users' group meeting that is planned for the next few weeks. Try not to lose momentum or interest from faculty.

Digital object users' groups

Facilitating digital object users' groups – a digital image user group and a digital video user group – serves several purposes for the repository team and for faculty. These groups create an informal focus group for the repository team. Use the forum as an opportunity to discuss issues that faculty are grappling with. Hear from them first hand rather than making assumptions. What are their biggest challenges in using digital objects? What has worked well for them? How are they incorporating digital objects into their teaching? What services could you provide that you aren't already?

These user group meetings also allow faculty to learn from each other and make new connections. Make sure that the sessions are about the faculty – and not a sales pitch by the library. Keep librarian attendance to a minimum; at the least, be sure that repository, library, and instructional technology staff do not outnumber faculty attendees.

At smaller institutions, organize events around a particular topic or type of object, i.e., create a digital image users' group and a separate digital video users' group. At larger institutions, it might work better to organize events around groups of disciplines – i.e., a session for humanities faculty, a separate session for sciences and engineering, and another for social sciences. While cross-fertilization of ideas occurs when faculty from multiple disciplines are together, it can be challenging to manage discussions in a particularly large group. Try different approaches and see what works best for your institution.

Meetings can be simple events. Send out an e-mail to all faculty or targeted groups of faculty and ask them to RSVP. It is not necessary to serve lunch or snacks – if faculty are interested, they'll attend regardless of whether or not food is served. Try to schedule a meeting at a time when few faculty are teaching, although no one time is ever ideal for all potential participants. Make it clear in the invitation sent out that the group is informal; attendees do not need to come to the session with a specialized set of knowledge or expertise, and they do not need to have participated in past meetings. See Figure 2.1, 'Sample invitation to video users' group' and Figure 2.2, 'Sample agenda for digital image users' group discussion' for details.

Someone from the repository team, ideally the coordinator, should facilitate the meeting, but try to get faculty talking to each other as much as possible. Have a set of questions prepared in advance to keep the discussion moving forward.

The sessions will likely introduce you to some potential partners, possibly some with whom the library has no prior relationship.

Workshops

Another approach to target faculty is to host workshops on specific topics of interest. A few workshops that often garner a great deal of enthusiasm from faculty:

- teaching with digital images;
- organizing personal collections workshop (images);
- teaching with digital video;
- student video projects;
- digital humanities scholarship;
- copyright and digital objects.

By partnering with an institutional technology group, you can structure a two-day workshop for faculty with various sessions related to teaching with digital objects, or you can create a one-day workshop specifically about issues related to digital scholarship and teaching with digital objects. See Figure 7.1, 'Workshop agenda,' for ideas for a day-long session. Such sessions can be held in January, before classes start again for the spring semester, or in May, immediately after classes are over but before Commencement. These two timeframes tend to work well for many schedules. Alternatively, you can hold one-hour sessions throughout

Figure 7.1	Workshop agenda

9:00–9:30	Overview, introductions
9:30–11:00	Teaching with digital objects *Presentations from three faculty members from three different disciplines about how they each use digital objects to support teaching.*
11:00–12:00	Personal collections *Hands-on session to learn how to use tools to better organize, describe, manage, and use your own images.*
12:00–1:00	Lunch
1:00–2:00	Introduction to digital video *Introductory hands-on session to learn how to shoot digital video by using video cameras, still cameras, phones, library equipment (available to use in classes), and other personal equipment.*
2:00–4:00	Introduction to video editing *Learn how to edit the video shot in the previous session by using software available on campus.*
4:00–4:45	Copyright issues Brief presentation followed by Q&A.
4:45–5:00	Concluding thoughts

the semester. These sessions should be repeated a few times to accommodate varying schedules, particularly if feedback from faculty is positive.

For any of these sessions, ask early adopters to lead workshops. Peer-led instruction is ideal for any group of learners, but it is particularly effective with faculty. Ask presenters to show student work if applicable.

Through all of these tactics, you will effectively be creating a community of practice, one that will benefit faculty who can make new connections to each other and the repository team who can learn from the faculty's experiences.

Other potential partners within the institution

Research centers, programs, and areas of excellence

The repository can be used as a means of supporting strategic areas of importance within an institution: highlighting materials from a new program or major, showcasing a research center, or bringing together scholarship from multiple disciplines. An 'environmental studies' collection, for example, can be used to pull together scholarship and objects from courses, faculty, and students in departments as varied as history, biology, anthropology, geography, geology, and chemistry. Many schools often have an environmental center; such a collection is an ideal way to showcase that research center, its programming, and its speakers.

Case study: event-based collections

Campus events – particularly high-profile events – can provide an excellent starting point for building a repository collection. At Bucknell University, the Digital Initiatives Group[1] created their initial institutional repository collection around Focus the Nation, a one-day national event tethered to environmental issues. As the abstract from the Coalition for Networked Information (CNI) Project Briefing for the Spring 2008 Task Force Meeting explains:

> Most of the literature related to creating an institutional repository program suggests starting small – either with one department or a project such as electronic theses and dissertations. Bucknell University took an entirely different approach in an attempt to get broader experience

by working with a cross-section of members of the university community and multiple types of digital objects all in one shot. This initial collection was built around Bucknell's participation in Focus the Nation, a one-day national teach-in held at colleges and universities designed to raise awareness about environmental issues. The resulting archive includes video and slide shows from faculty presentations, digital images taken of students and faculty with exhibits, electronic copies of research posters, and other relevant materials.[2]

This collection allowed the repository team to work with a variety of content types, a cross-section of the campus community, and to support a high-profile campus event – all of which were extremely beneficial learning experiences. Furthermore, event-oriented collections have a discrete starting and stopping point; the project has a limited length of time, which was helpful to quickly jump-start a repository program. By working towards a goal with an immovable date, it gave the team an impetus to quickly negotiate a non-exclusive license with the university counsel's office, a license that was then used as a template moving forward for other areas of the repository.

By including video of presentations, question and answer sessions from faculty panels, and trying to include video of guest speakers in the repository, a number of unexpected issues were uncovered as well. What to do with presentations that included slides containing images that were not in the public domain? How to simultaneously capture both the faculty member speaking and the slides being displayed? Is it possible to add language to an existing contract for an outside speaker to include language granting permission to the repository to deposit video of his presentation and make that video publicly accessible?

While the focus of this project was on capturing the university's experiences at this particular event, it created an opportunity to try to work with libraries at other institutions as well. At that point, Bucknell was participating in the NITLE DSpace Repository,[3] an instance of DSpace that was used to host collections at approximately 20 mainly small, liberal arts institutions. Representatives from several other institutions expressed interest in creating a joint collection of digital objects related to the 2008 Focus the Nation event. While a common collection did not come to fruition, the conversations were productive in raising policy issues and technical questions that were helpful to frame future discussions related to creating multi-institutional collections.

The development office

Development or fundraising offices can be unexpected potential partners. Development officers are often looking for new and interesting projects for which they can look for funding sources, and digital repository projects have the benefit of being considered 'sexy' – their graphics and visuals provide a good hook. Meet with a representative of the development office on a regular basis to keep them apprised of current projects, the type of collections that the repository program supports, and potential opportunities for donors.

What to show before you have collections

It is far easier to discuss digital collections when you have some examples to show, particularly examples that are relevant to your audience, which poses an interesting dilemma before your repository has its own collections. During this phase, the best approach is to find a handful of collections from peer and aspirant institutions that represent a good sample pool, ideally samples that are using the same system in use at your institution. When meeting with someone from the art gallery, show them examples from similar-sized, similar-profile institutions. If you are a small institution, don't show your audience a collection from a large, well-funded institution. Try to compare apples to apples – you don't want to inflate the perception of what a finished collection at your institution might look like.

For faculty or journal editors, try to share examples from the same (or related) disciplines. Faculty often think that their discipline is vastly different from another discipline, so try to show examples that are as closely-tied to their area of study as possible.

Recruiting content from outside of the university

Working outside of the university presents unlimited possibilities for recruiting new content and developing partnerships. However, be careful that projects stay within the boundaries set out in the program's strategic plan. If your program has specified that it will support collections that are clearly tied to the curriculum, you need to ensure that there is an internal demand for the collection and that it will be used by members of the campus community. The best way to ensure this link is to find a faculty partner who will participate in the project and will use it in a course. Otherwise, you run the risk of creating a collection that is difficult to justify supporting.

Big and small ways to market your repository program

Marketing efforts don't need to be big to be successful, although all marketing plans should be thoughtful in their approach. What are you trying to accomplish? What's the best way to accomplish that objective? Following are a few approaches that demonstrate various levels of investment in terms of both time and money. These suggestions are geared towards showcasing the program as a whole by driving users to the site and generating broad interest. For details on using Web 2.0 tools, see Chapter 11, 'Web 2.0 and digital repositories.'

Developing a promotion plan

As part of the project implementation, develop and implement a promotion plan to advertise your collection. Promotion is the method of alerting your targeted audience to a new product or service, in this case, the collection. Take advantage of promotional materials others have designed. DSpace, Fedora, and ePrints all have promotional materials posted on their websites. When advertising the collection or the repository program itself, language is critically important. Be sure to use words and phrases that are meaningful to faculty – not library-specific jargon.

Build-your-own collection[4]

Have the campus work together to create a collection. Come up with a loose idea for a theme and open up the collection to the entire campus – or possibly, alumni and the broader community. Sample ideas include travel, study abroad, favorite local locations, animals, pets; or try something more abstract – a noun or a verb: flowers, shapes, seasons, teaching, love, pride, or trust. The collection could be a contest, with a group of finalists voted upon by the campus. If there is funding for the project, host a dinner or open house for participants. Approach the art department and art gallery to co-sponsor the collection. The two objectives for such a project:

1. Get the campus community invested in the repository project.
2. Showcase other collections: when people go to see the collection, they will inevitably be exposed to other collections. Take advantage of this interest and draw in new users to existing collections.

When building such a collection, it is important to include a few dozen objects at the collection's launch. Create an easy-to-use submission process so participants can upload metadata, permissions, and their objects via a web form. Be prepared to put some limits (x uploads per person) and restrictions into effect.

Screensavers

An extremely simple, low-tech way to advertise content from collections is to create screensavers with photos from collections. At Emory University,[5] the standard computer image for the library includes screensavers that showcase various images from collections created at the institution. This inexpensive, low-tech tool introduces students (and the public) to materials from collections they might not know existed. It is a simple way to increase exposure to collections.

Newsletters

Another inexpensive way to share news about your collection is to create a newsletter to distribute to those who register or express interest. Set up a blog on your website with a subscription to the site that allows subscribers to be notified every time a post is added to the site. Google's Feedburner is a simple and free way to set up blog subscriptions.

Newsletters – ones that can be printed out to display or mail – are a more involved option. Even if newsletters are not going to be mailed to readers, create a formal presence for the repository program. If a library already has a newsletter, write a regular column updating the community on new collections, proposal deadlines, and upcoming events.

Within the professional LIS community

The library/information science community is full of avenues for advertising your program and individual collections within it. *D-Lib Magazine* includes a featured collection[6] in each issue. The Association of College and Research Libraries' (ACRL) journal *College and Research Library News*[7] regularly looks for images to publish on the cover of its journal. Submit an image from one of your publicly available collections. Take advantage of the multitude of listservs within the LIS community. Whenever you launch a new publicly available collection, post a message to relevant listservs.

Digital collections are ideally suited for poster sessions at conferences. Even if the project followed standard best practices and did not break any new ground in terms of digital library systems or workflows, librarians are always interested in being exposed to new collections. What is the collection? How is it being used? Talk about your experiences at conferences or write an article. Many professional journals have special theme issues on a regular basis related to digital repositories.

Showcasing individual projects and collections

Make a point to announce individual projects and collections, particularly those that are publicly accessible. Write and distribute press releases to appropriate campus, local, or national news outlets. Contact the student newspaper and invite them to interview the project manager or content owner about the collection once a project has been launched. Submit articles or brief announcements to the university's alumni magazine, the library's newsletter, and publications such as the *Chronicle of Higher Education*. Target the professional community for the discipline tied to the project. For instance, submit announcements or press releases to journals, listservs, and websites related to the professional chemistry community, mathematics education practitioners, or historians. If the collection is appropriate for K-12 students, broadly target those teachers as well.

Notes

1. The Bucknell University Digital Initiatives Group circa 2008 consisted of Abby Clobridge (Digital Initiatives Group Leader), Laura Riskedahl (Metadata Librarian), and Daniel Mancusi (Digital Projects Technologist). At that point, the Digital Initiatives Group was under the leadership of Nancy Dagle, Director of Library Services.
2. Clobridge, A. (2008). *Starting an institutional repository program in two months or less: The good, the bad, and the ugly.* Project briefing: Spring 2008 task force meeting. Retrieved January 5, 2010 from http://www.cni.org/tfms/2008a.spring/abstracts/PB-starting-clobridge.html
3. *DSpace* (n.d.). Retrieved January 5, 2010 from http://dspace.nitle.org

4. While we never got an opportunity to put this idea into action, Mike Weaver and the rest of the instructional technology team at Bucknell University were responsible for its genesis. Before I left Bucknell, we had planned to implement such a collection with the theme of geometry.

5. Author site visit to Emory University, August 2008.

6. Gueguen, G. (2009). Featured collection: Joyner Library digital collections. *D-Lib Magazine*, **15**(7–8). Retrieved January 5, 2010 from http://www.dlib.org/dlib/july09/07featured-collection.html

7. *College and Research Libraries News* (n.d.). Instructions for authors. Retrieved on January 5, 2010 from http://crln.acrl.org/site/misc/author.xhtml

8

Open Access

Introduction: what is open access?

In a nutshell, open access is a form of scholarly publishing in which materials are 'digital, online, free of charge, and free of most copyright and licensing restrictions.'[1] The Budapest Open Access Initiative (BOAI), one of the original efforts to codify and support open access in a formulaic way, defined open access as scholarly articles that have:

> free availability on the public internet, permitting any users to read, download, copy, distribute, print, search, or link to the full texts of these articles, crawl them for indexing, pass them as data to software, or use them for any other lawful purpose, without financial, legal, or technical barriers other than those inseparable from gaining access to the internet itself. The only constraint on reproduction and distribution, and the only role for copyright in this domain, should be to give authors control over the integrity of their work and the right to be properly acknowledged and cited.[2]

Open access refers first and foremost to peer-reviewed scholarly articles; other types of materials such as news articles, chapters, books, born-digital multimedia projects, supplemental data sets, and un-refereed articles are not included in formal definitions of open access, although these materials are generally welcome in open access repositories.

The initial push for open access was to make research more widely, freely, and quickly accessible to the world – to increase the potential impact factor for research. But there are financial issues that are intertwined with this goal. With skyrocketing costs of journals and quickly shrinking budgets, academic libraries are becoming interested in supporting open access for financial reasons as well. Even without increasing costs, no library is able to purchase all articles from all journals. Researchers at institutions with limited budgets cannot provide access to the wealth of scholarship being produced, much of it funded by public dollars.[3] However, this second problem, that of journal affordability, is mainly a library issue. It has implications for researchers, but it is not a terribly effective way to get faculty interested in open access.

Several recent articles and books have explored a variety of issues related to open access. Catherine Jones, in *Institutional repositories: Content and culture in an open access environment*,[4] looks at repositories specifically through the lens of supporting open access work. A theme issue of *Library Trends* in 2008 was dedicated to institutional repositories. See Neil Jacobs, Amber Thomas, and Andrew McGregor's article, 'Institutional repositories in the UK: The JISC approach'[5] and Carole L. Palmer, Lauren C. Teffeau, and Mark P. Newton's article, 'Strategies for institutional repository development: A case study of three evolving initiatives.'[6] For ideas about promoting an institutional repository to faculty, see Miguel Ferriera, Ana Alice Baptista, Eloy Rodrigues, and Ricardo Saraiva's article, 'Carrots and sticks: Some ideas on how to create a successful institutional repository.'[7]

Open access has the potential to have a significant impact on researchers, faculty, publishers, and libraries. With declining revenues, loss of control over how intellectual property is used, misperceptions about copyright and open access, changes in workflows and services, open access can be a highly contentious issue on campus.

Guiding principles

Some overarching principles to keep in mind when moving forward with open access:

Open access mandates can be useful, but they aren't the only way.
Don't wait for a mandate that may never be adopted before talking to faculty about open access. Some institutions fare well without a mandate – it depends on the culture of the institution and the library.

When working with researchers or faculty, sell how open access can help them.
Talk about the 'opening of access' to their research, wider dissemination, expanded access to their work – rather than 'open access.' Focus on increased access to their articles, leading to higher impact.

Most challenges with open access are related to policy and process, not technology.
Those who are acting as advocates for open access within the campus community should have a solid understanding of the issues tied to supporting open access. What services are in place? What are the long-term issues? Present a realistic, reasonable perspective when talking to faculty. Be prepared.

Open access is one facet of a repository program.
From the library's perspective, think about supporting open access as a core set of services tied to the repository program – not a separate program in itself. Open access should fit in with the strategic plan for your institution's repository program.

Misperceptions and misinformation about open access are abundant.
Library staff members need to be prepared to answer questions and be comfortable with ambiguity. While digital repositories have been increasingly common since the late 1990s, open access mandates create a stark change for faculty members.

Nuts and bolts of open access

There are two routes to open access: green open access (self-archiving) and gold open access publishing. The two routes are vastly different from each other, although they are not mutually exclusive.

In green open access, authors publish in the scholarly, peer-reviewed journal of their choice. During the copyright transfer process, they secure rights to deposit a version of their articles in an open access repository or post on a personal website. After the article has been accepted, authors then 'self archive' (i.e., post/deposit) the agreed-upon version of the article, usually a pre-print. Currently, many journals automatically grant authors the right to deposit/post their articles, but only a small percentage of authors do so.

Many journals are beginning to include self-archiving permission as part of the standard copyright agreement. The SHERPA/RoMEO Project includes a searchable database of scholarly journals and their copyright policies for self-archiving pre-prints and post-prints.[8] As part of the standard process to submit articles for publication, authors still transfer all copyright over to the journal. The only difference is that they retain the right to self-archive – and, in some instances, to migrate the format of documents in the future as file formats become obsolete (i.e., to convert from Microsoft Word 2003 to Microsoft Word 2007).

In gold open access, authors publish their articles directly in peer-reviewed open access journals. The Directory of Open Access Journals (DOAJ)[9] maintains a list of such journals that follow the BOAI definition of open access (see above), have an editorial board or use peer-reviewers, and are primarily research-oriented. Furthermore, they must meet the following criteria:[10]

Selection criteria (for inclusion in the Directory of Open Access Journals):

Coverage:

- Subject: all scientific and scholarly subjects are covered.
- Types of resource: scientific and scholarly periodicals that publish research or review papers in full text.
- Acceptable sources: academic, government, commercial, non-profit private sources are all acceptable.
- Level: the target group for included journals should be primarily researchers.
- Content: a substantive part of the journal should consist of research papers. All content should be available in full text.
- All languages.

Access:

- All content freely available.
- Registration: Free user registration online is acceptable.
- Open access without delay (e.g. no embargo period).

Quality:

Quality control: for a journal to be included it should exercise quality control on submitted papers through an editor, editorial board and/or a peer-review system.

Periodical:

The journal should have an ISSN (International Standard Serial Number, for information see http://www.issn.org).

Open access journals are freely and globally accessible, so all of their articles are as well. However, many 'gold' open access journals are running into financial difficulties. Since they are not charging for individual or institutional subscriptions, they need to come up with alternate ways to generate operating funds.

If the ultimate goal is to make research immediately and freely accessible to a global audience, either route succeeds.

Open access mandates

Increasingly, funding organizations, entire universities, and departments are passing mandates that require individuals to deposit copies of articles into open access repositories. Each mandate has its own terms, and many use criteria set out by the BOAI to define what is covered by the mandate. However, some institutions or departments broaden the definition to include chapters in edited books.

Organizations such as the National Institute of Health (NIH) in the United States have begun to mandate for open access as well. In these cases, individuals who receive funding from those particular organizations are required to deposit copies of articles containing research sponsored by their funds in open access repositories.

The Registry of Open Access Repository Material Archiving Policies (ROARMAP) website[11] maintains a global list of policies, institutions, and URLs with relevant information.

Clarifying common misconceptions

Open access stirs up a number of debates, often with faculty who are understandably concerned about their intellectual property and scholarly output. Below are some notes to help dispel some myths and misconceptions about open access.

1. Open access is not open source

Open-source software is a type of computer software for which the authors of the source code grant users the rights to 'use, change, and improve the software, and to redistribute it in modified or unmodified forms.'[12]

Open access, on the other hand, is entirely about free, immediate, global access to research. All rights traditionally associated with scholarship are retained by the copyright holder, most often, journal publishers. For articles that are published in non-open access journals, authors seek permission to 'self-archive' by posting a copy of the article to their personal websites or depositing a copy in an open access repository. Many publishers automatically grant this permission; still others will allow self-archiving if authors request it in the form of an author addenda to the copyright license. All other rights associated with articles remain with publishers.

2. Open access does not fundamentally change copyright ownership. Open source articles are not in the public domain

Open access itself has no bearing on the rights associated with a particular article. However, in order to deposit an article in an open access repository, the author needs to have permission to do so either by:

- publishing the article in an open access journal that automatically grants self-archiving privileges;

- publishing the article in a traditional journal that grants permission to self-archive;

- negotiate self-archiving privileges as part of the copyright transfer process.

In any of these cases, the publisher still owns all rights to articles in their journals, unless negotiated otherwise. In these cases, the publisher has granted permission to deposit – not given up any further rights.

3. Open access, by its definition, is only referring to peer-reviewed, scholarly articles

While repositories often accept (and encourage) other types of scholarship such as student theses, chapters from books, and data sets, the definition of open access limits the body of scholarship to articles.

4. To achieve open access, an author does not need to publish in an open access journal

While there are indeed two routes to achieving open access, 'green' open access is often overlooked or forgotten about.

Along with the substantial recent rise in OA consciousness worldwide, there has also been an unfortunate tendency to equate OA exclusively with OA journal publishing (i.e., the golden road to OA) and to overlook the faster, surer, and already more heavily traveled green road of OA self-archiving. This oversight is probably a spin-off of conflating the journal-affordability problem with the access/impact problem.[13]

5. Open access journals use editorial boards, peer-reviewers, and editors

Open access journals – and non-open access journals that allow open access self-archiving – all must meet the criteria set out by the Budapest Open Access Initiative (BOAI) to be considered true open access. They must be scholarly in nature, have an editorial board or editors, and use peer-reviewers.

What does OA mean for libraries?

Open access provides new opportunities for libraries and staff. Library administrators can lead discussions on campus about open access and the benefits of depositing scholarship in digital repositories. Librarians at campuses with OA mandates or where there is significant interest among faculty to deposit materials in repositories can use the opportunity to provide outreach for the repository program and serve as liaisons for open access.

Repositories – particularly in conjunction with open access movements – can also create more formal opportunities for librarians to become involved throughout the research process. While librarians have always been involved in work throughout the information lifecycle, open access creates new ways to draw upon our expertise and support researchers.

But open access repositories – particularly at institutions with mandates – are not necessarily a good thing for libraries. Ideally, a repository and trained staff should be in place before a mandate is passed. Mandates that are driven by faculty without strong library involvement can lead to challenges. If a mandate is passed without a repository, repository staff, or repository services in place, the institution will have a difficult time properly supporting the mandate. Library-run institutional repositories should be properly planned, resourced, and staffed – and not thrown together as a reaction to a mandate.[14]

Supporting mandates from funding organizations

Strategies to support open access do not need to be complicated or expensive. At the University of Nebraska, Lincoln, the library partnered with the Office of Research Compliance to support researchers who received NIH grants.[15] With minimal programming, the two departments set up an automated system. As soon as faculty members receive a grant from NIH, they receive an e-mail with information about the NIH Public Access Policy. The message informs them that scientists are required to deposit a copy of all peer-reviewed journal manuscripts related to research that received NIH funding in PubMed Central, the NIH's free digital archive. The message provides links to resources, including contact information of a librarian who can answer questions or help with the deposit process. Faculty receive a few additional follow-up automated e-mails throughout the duration of their grant award.[16]

The University of Nebraska does not have an open access mandate and therefore does not require faculty to put copies of manuscripts to be deposited in their own repository. Even so, the NIH mandate provides opportunities to talk to faculty about open access, the university's digital repository, and the general benefits of depositing their scholarship into an OA repository.

Supporting faculty workflow for repository submissions

A theme running throughout open access repository work is the notion of 'self-submission,' an idea that sounds good in theory but does not work well in practice. A key decision for the library is whether or not it will voluntarily take on this work and handle the deposit process on behalf of faculty. If not, it is more likely that faculty, research, or departmental assistants will be the ones depositing materials. Getting the library involved leads to more consistent metadata, gives staff an opportunity to support faculty research in new ways, and allows staff to be more aware of what faculty are publishing, which can improve collection development work. Librarians already have relationships with publishers and should have a level of expertise in copyright. Library staff should also be aware of new tools and other developments such as the RoMEO project that can support this process.

Supporting the publishing process

At the least, librarians should be prepared to be more engaged in discussions with researchers – faculty, staff, and students – about the publishing process. The transition from print publishing to digital publishing has created a far more complex environment, which raises new questions for experienced authors and often leaves new authors in need of support. Expect liaison librarians to be able to answer questions or designate a specific librarian to serve as a coordinator/ supporter for scholarly communication issues.

Typical questions:

■ How do I deposit my article into PubMed Central?

- How do I know if I have to deposit my article into PubMed Central?

- Which version of my article do I submit?

- What rights do I automatically have as an author once I submit an article to be published?

- How do I get permission from a publisher to deposit articles I wrote into a repository or post something to my personal website? Is it too late to ask for permission once an article has been published?

- What does it mean to publish in an open access journal?

- What are some open access journals in my discipline?

- What is the impact factor for a particular journal?

- How can I tell what databases a particular journal is indexed in?

- How do I get a Creative Commons license? Which one do I want to use?

- If I publish in an open access journal, will it hurt my chances for tenure?

When working with graduate students or undergraduate researchers, they also have questions such as:

- What's involved in submitting proposals to journals? Do I need to submit an abstract or a full article?

- How to select journals to submit proposals to in a particular field?

- How long does the review process take?

- What's involved in the review process?

These issues will continue to get more complex, not less. It is imperative that librarians have a solid understanding of the issues.

Selling open access

For researchers, the major advantage of open access is the potential increase in impact of their scholarship. Articles in open access repositories are indexed by search engines. The metadata associated with records (authors' names, abstract, assigned subject terms/keywords) and the full-text versions of articles themselves are crawled by all of the major search engines and will appear in search results. Internet searchers – even if they are not specifically looking for articles – are driven to repository results. If a researcher's objective is to have his or her scholarship read, then making it more widely accessible by posting it on the Internet is an easy way to potentially expand readership and exposure. There is no way to realistically measure readership of articles in printed journals; electronic journal page views are measured by publishers, but they do not share that information with article authors. Within repositories, it is easy to collect and provide page view and download statistics to authors. Ideally, journals provide one set of services (peer review, article selection and rejection, organization, crafting of scholarship within a specific niche, marketing, credibility, etc.) and the repository provides another, complementary set of services.

Another selling point for faculty to participate in repositories has been author pages. Faculty can post information about themselves and their current research projects; make slideshows and presentations available; provide links to personal websites, conferences, or organizations with which they are affiliated, all in a way that is presented in connection to their articles. While most journals include a statement about the author or a one-paragraph biography, the repository can host far more information and can be updated and expanded over time. Faculty can have control over their profiles and can include links to all types of materials.

Departments and institutions can potentially benefit from showcasing their researchers' scholarly output in the form of an open access repository. Grant reviewers may be more inclined to accept a proposal after reviewing the scholarship in a particular department or by an individual. Prospective students can also review scholarship by faculty or other students in a deeper way than is possible by reviewing CVs. Posting the research output of an institution can make it easier to differentiate among peer institutions.

Notes

1. Suber, P. (2007). *Open access overview*. Retrieved January 18, 2010 from http://www.earlham.edu/~peters/fos/overview.htm
2. Budapest open access initiative: Frequently asked questions (2009). Retrieved January 17, 2010 from http://www.earlham.edu/~peters/fos/boaifaq.htm
3. Harnad, S., Brody, T., Vallieres, F., Carr, L., Hitchcock, S., Gingras, Y., et al. (2004). The access/impact problem and the green and gold roads to open access. *Serials Review*, 30(4). Retrieved on January 18, 2010 from http://eprints.ecs.soton.ac.uk/10209
4. Jones, C. (2007). *Institutional repositories: Content and culture in an open access environment*. Oxford, UK: Chandos Publishing.
5. Jacobs, N., Thomas, A., and McGregor, A. (2008) Institutional repositories in the UK: The JISC approach. *Library Trends*, 57(2), 124–141.
6. Palmer, C., Teffeau, L., and Newton, M. (2008) Strategies for institutional repository development: A case study of three evolving initiatives. *Library Trends*, 57(2), 142–167.
7. Ferreira, M., Baptista, A., Rodrigues, E., and Saraiva, R. (2008) Carrots and sticks: Some ideas on how to create a successful institutional repository. *D-Lib Magazine* 14(12). Retrieved on December 19, 2009 from http://www.dlib.org/dlib/january08/ferreira/01ferreira.html
8. SHERPA RoMEO (n.d.). Retrieved on January 18, 2010 from http://www.sherpa.ac.uk/romeo/

9. Directory of open access journals (n.d.). Retrieved on January 18, 2010 from http://www.doaj.org/

10. Directory of open access journals (n.d.). Selection criteria. Retrieved on January 18, 2010 from http://www.doaj.org/doaj?func=loadTempl&templ=about#criteria

11. ePrints (n.d.). ROARMAP. Retrieved on January 18, 2010 from http://www.eprints.org/openaccess/policysignup/

12. Wikipedia(n.d.). Open source. http://en.wikipedia.org/wiki/Open_source

13. Harnad, S., Brody, T., Vallieres, F., Carr, L., Hitchcock, S., Gingras, Y., et al. (2004). The access/impact problem and the green and gold roads to open access. *Serials Review*, 30(4). Retrieved on January 18, 2010 from http://eprints.ecs.soton.ac.uk/10209

14. Salo, D. (2008). Innkeeper at the roach motel. *Library Trends*, 57(2), 98–123.

15. Gieseckie, J. (2008). NIH public access policy: Campus implementation strategies. *Proceedings of the 152nd ARL Membership Meeting*. Retrieved on January 22, 2010 from http://www.arl.org/resources/pubs/mmproceedings/152mm-proceedings.shtml

16. Gieseckie, J. (2008). NIH public access policy: Campus implementation strategies. *Proceedings of the 152nd ARL Membership Meeting*. Retrieved on January 22, 2010 from http://www.arl.org/resources/pubs/mmproceedings/152mm-proceedings.shtml

9

Sustainability

Introduction

Long-term sustainability of digital programs, collections, and objects is one of the biggest question marks in repository work. Although practitioners all acknowledge that digital preservation is a major concern, most work related to digital preservation is still at the research or theoretical level. Few strategies have had widespread adoption, particularly among smaller institutions. However, no institution can afford to completely ignore preservation issues while others work to 'solve' the problem – and it would be irresponsible to do so.

The preservation challenges created by shifting to a digital environment are significant. Issues include dealing with file format, hardware and software obsolescence; investing in dark archives; releasing embargoed objects; and working with rights issues related to reformatting. At a higher level, which is where most of the real challenges lie, how is born-digital culture being captured and preserved? What is the role of libraries to collect and curate born-digital content (not necessarily scholarship) that is created outside of the university's infrastructure – content such as websites, blogs, and Twitter posts? How can libraries collect and curate cultural materials and ephemera from communities in a way parallel to how we captured those materials in the analog world? What role will we define in this sphere for academic libraries? How can we support collecting such information produced by and about our institutions?

Elsewhere in the library, staff are grappling with another issue related to digital preservation, one tied to the model of acquiring digital content from publishers. In the analog environment, books are purchased outright. Libraries then own in perpetuity those particular items. Digital content, on the other hand, is licensed. Libraries pay to 'lease' time-limited access to objects including electronic journals and increasingly books for e-readers. In most cases, libraries never hold a copy of the objects themselves; copies are retained by the publisher or distributor. Libraries then provide indirect access to the objects via publishers' websites.

This new model drastically changes how we think about digital content, what libraries own, and how to build and maintain collections. Digital repository teams are often advocates for digital preservation, but all librarians should be concerned about, and well versed in, the issues. Services such as LOCKSS can provide an opportunity for a different group of library staff members to become involved in issues related to digital preservation. These issues related to content acquisition, licensing, and collection development are much larger than repository programs.

Preservation of digital objects is just one facet of maintaining the long-term health of a repository program. While it is the largest cloud looming over many repositories, it is critical to consider sustainability of collections, the program team, and commitment to the program itself. If collections are transient, it will become more challenging to maintain content owners' support. Without a solid repository team, the program will falter. And without long-term support from the administration, a solid program can easily vanish. Repository programs require a significant commitment from the library's administration; one should be created only if the administration intends to support it for many years to come.

This chapter focuses mainly on strategies for sustaining digital objects within repositories, digital collections, repository teams, and the program itself.

Guiding principles

Don't wait.
While there aren't simple solutions to the big digital preservation issues yet, there are plenty of small strategies to put into effect immediately to preserve materials in repositories and other targeted groups of digital objects.

Not all collections should be treated equally.
Communicate clearly with content owners so their expectations for preservation and long-term access are properly managed.

Maintaining the health of the repository and the program is an ongoing effort.
Invest in the program, its staff, and maintain the support of library administrators on an ongoing basis. Don't assume the program will still be there in five years; make it a critical, strategic part of the library – one that can't be cut.

Sustaining digital objects

Digital objects within repositories

Repository managers need to take responsibility for maintaining and preserving the digital objects that are under their care. Some activities associated with digital preservation are necessary for every institution, even those with limited resources. These activities include backing up files, determining the levels of support for various file types, and some degree of disaster planning. Other activities related to digital preservation may not be necessary for every institution. Some questions to consider:

- What will be preserved? Everything? Selected collections? Everything that meets certain criteria?

- What file formats will be accepted into the repository?

- Are you preserving access to the file (i.e., access to its bits and bytes) or promising usable, workable access to the file?

- What is the plan for backing up data and digital objects stored in the repository?

Answers to these questions will determine what types of preservation services the repository program will need to support and how to craft messages about preservation.

Backups

Having a tested backup plan is imperative for all repository programs. Repository managers and systems administrators should work together to craft and test a plan. Who is responsible for backing up files in the repository? How often does it occur? What format is used for the backups? How long are backups maintained? As part of the process to create a backup plan, try to fully restore the repository database from a backup and document this process in great detail.

Obsolete formats, software, and hardware

File formats, hardware, and software becoming obsolete cause issues for all repository managers. A common strategy employed by many institutions but modeled after MIT's policy[1] is to accept all file types, provide access to all file types, but only 'support' certain types of file formats. Under this model, the repository plans to provide full support, including file migration, for formats built on open standards. MIT maintains a DSpace Format Reference Collection,[2] a list of file formats, their formats, and the level of support the repository team will provide for each format. This list is often adapted by institutions for their repositories, regardless of whether the repository is using DSpace or not.

In this model, proprietary formats (including many commonly-used formats) are 'known' but not fully supported. This means that these formats are recognized but the repository team will not guarantee that they will be able to migrate files to usable formats in the future. Readability of proprietary file formats is in large part dependent upon the format owner. Open formats, on the other hand, are built on international standards.

Another strategy is to limit repositories to only accept open formats. While open formats are preferred, not accepting other formats will present many long-term problems. Many documents are created in proprietary formats. The digital archive then either ignores this corpus of material, creating a skewed snapshot of university files, or files are required to be converted to other types. The conversion process can be as simple and straightforward as converting a word processing document to a PDF. But complex documents may lose some layers or functionality from the original document. For example, a word processing document that includes embedded audio and video or files including tracked changes may lose some of this additional construction in the conversion process. Flattening AutoCAD files into tiffs will likely lose some layers.

For open file formats, preservation means refreshing files on a regular basis to ensure that they are still intact, and paying attention to file formats as they become obsolete. As formats do become obsolete, the repository team will need to update/migrate files as this happens. For most file types, this will mean converting large batches of files at once.

In addition to file formats becoming obsolete, repository teams need to pay attention to hardware and software becoming obsolete. For instance, finding hardware to play eight-track cassettes, cassettes, records, 8" disks, 5 ¼" floppy disks, and even 3 ½" floppy disks can be difficult. At some point, finding hardware to play CDs and DVDs will also be challenging.

Disaster planning

Natural disasters can do a great deal of damage to campuses. Even localized events such as floods, leaks, and fires can ruin servers and have a significant impact on libraries. The extent of a repository program's plan for disaster recovery should be proportionate to the importance of the materials stored in the repository. If a repository is storing critically important business files, off-site storage is appropriate. But for repository programs with far more modest goals, redundancy among servers might be sufficient. Most programs fall somewhere between the two extremes, and the repository steering group should create a plan appropriate for the goals of the program.

Mirror sites or exchanging backups on a regularly scheduled basis with a peer institution are two viable options. One organization providing such a service in a formal way is MetaArchive, a cooperative digital preservation effort in the United States, which supports private networks of digital objects by 'dynamically replicating and distributing them to multiple file servers in multiple locations.'[3] Institutions can also make arrangements with each other to swap backups or host mirrors for each other.

Crafting a clear message

Clearly communicate with content owners. What are you promising them? In 15 years, will their grandchildren be able to read the documents they submitted? Repository teams need to ensure that faculty who are depositing materials into open access repositories and content owners who are building collections have appropriate expectations. Not all collections or content must be treated equally, but all content owners should know what preservation services will be applied to their materials.

Electronic records management

While electronic records management is becoming an increasing concern for many institutions, the library is often not involved in planning for or implementing a strategy to support administrative electronic records. However, the work is very similar in nature to repository work, and the administrative systems team should take advantage of the repository team's expertise in curating digital objects and working with metadata. See Figure 9.1, 'Digital curation for electronic records management: long-term preservation and accessibility,' for a sample case statement.

Additional topics in digital preservation

The above work should be undertaken by all institutions, even those with the smallest budgets for digital repositories. For those institutions interested in going further with digital

Figure 9.1	Digital curation for electronic records management: long-term preservation and accessibility

Digital curation consists of a suite of services working in tandem to ensure long-term usability of digital objects stored in a repository. The two overarching sets of services deal with long-term preservation (storage of the objects themselves) and accessibility (making sure the digital objects are able to be used in the future). In essence, services need to be provided to ensure that digital content will remain viable and accessible in the future – despite constant changes in technology.

Examples of digital curation services:

- providing secure storage for digital objects including: providing redundancy and file back-ups, running checksums (reviewing the integrity of data/files over time), refreshing data by periodically moving files;
- supporting systems designed to deliver digital objects to end users;
- ensuring long-term preservation of digital objects by migrating files as formats become obsolete;
- providing tools to monitor data about collections and usage.

Examples of responsibilities of content owners:

- maintaining disposition schedules;
- providing necessary metadata about each object.

Supporting a repository for electronic records management requires long-term commitment from an institution in terms of continued funding for servers, systems, other resources, and policies. Beginning an electronic records program requires changes in workflows for content owners, as materials need to be submitted to a repository (or repository managers) in a timely fashion. Furthermore, submitted materials must include relevant data – descriptive information about the object itself, but also information providing insight into the how, when, and who of records creation. Without this information, digital objects will not be useable or useful in the future. Policies emphasizing the importance of a university-wide electronic records program need to be mandated from university management, not from the library, in order for the campus to be successful.

preservation, investigate the Open Archival Information System (OAIS) Reference Model,[4] the PREMIS Data Dictionary,[5] the RLG-OCLC Audit Checklist for Certifying Digital Repositories,[6] and services to verify content integrity of digital objects.

Curation of digital objects outside of universities

The focus of most academic libraries' digital preservation work should be directly tied to objects in their repositories. But because digital preservation issues are so intertwined, it is natural to be involved in much broader issues as well – and it is a strategic move for the library or repository team to take a leadership position within the institution as a resource in all digital preservation issues, issues including archiving websites, preservation of personal digital materials, and electronic records management.

The Library of Congress and DigitalPreservationEurope are both involved in producing and disseminating information about digital preservation aimed at raising awareness of digital preservation issues among the general public and are producing resources that might be of value or interest to members of the university community. The Library of Congress's National Digital Information Infrastructure and Preservation Program (NDIIPP) was designed to 'develop a national strategy to collect, preserve and make available significant digital content, especially information that is created in digital form only, for current and future generations.'[7] NDIIPP maintains an inventory of tools and services[8] designed to support digital preservation created by members of its global network of partners. Tools support a wide area of interests such as data integrity, website archives, data set archives, web crawling, and geospatial information systems (GIS).

DigitalPreservationEurope[9] (DPE) has developed a number of humorous animated videos designed to raise awareness about digital preservation. The cartoon series stars Team Digital Preservation and DigiMan and is hosted on YouTube on the WePreserve Channel.[10] A second campaign designed to get the public interested in digital preservation is the Digital Preservation Challenge, a contest for students. 'The challenge is to develop digital preservation solutions that overcome the barriers hindering three digital objects, each accompanied by a scenario based on real-life situations: Electronic art, Webarchiving and Unknown files.'[11] Cash prizes were awarded to three winners.

University-created materials hosted elsewhere on the Internet

Universities have been creating websites since the 1990s, although few institutions have complete collections of their own sites. The Internet Archive[12] creates snapshots of websites and provides free access to them, creating an archive of the Internet itself. Since the objective is to archive the Internet as a whole, the focus is on the big picture, not capturing daily updates to individual websites. Snapshots of sites are sporadic and usually only go a few levels into a given site. While it is an excellent resource and has prevented the complete loss of any record for most institutions' websites, it should not be the only archive for institutions' websites. Some department on campus – either the archive, the library as a whole, or a repository team – should be assigned responsibility for archiving pre-selected parts or all of a university's official website on a regular schedule. Tools such as HTTrack[13] can be used for this purpose; HTTrack allows users to download all or parts of a website, including images and other files, to a local directory.

In addition to hosting websites, most academic institutions also have an online presence in YouTube, Facebook, Twitter, and Flickr, with new social network sites popping up on a regular basis. Who is collecting and preserving the information your institution is formally posting? Is the dialogue with students, alumni, prospective students, and other communities being captured and preserved? Services such as backupify[14] are designed to create backups or archives of online accounts. Is online backup of cloud-based accounts a role the library, repository program, or archive should take on for your institution?

Although IT, public relations, or communications departments maintain the official online presence for institutions, many members of the university community also write and maintain websites, some of which might be appropriate content for an academic library to identify, archive, and maintain. For example, if a library collects faculty publications and manuscripts, should the library also identify, select, collect, archive, and preserve faculty blogs or course-based blog and wiki projects?

Curation of licensed digital content

While only a few librarians are directly involved in digital repository work at most institutions, all librarians have direct ties to electronic resources, i.e., databases and journals licensed from vendors. These resources are hosted by the vendor and linked to from libraries' websites, which presents an entirely different set of challenges in terms of digital preservation. What happens if a journal or a vendor goes out of business? In the digital world, access to those publications disappears. In the analog world, libraries can retain journals for as long as they want. Likewise, if a library decides to cease its subscription to a printed journal, the library doesn't send back previous issues to the publisher. The library owns the copies of the journals that it bought. In the digital world, libraries pay for limited access to journals. If a library ceases its subscription to an electronic journal or database, it loses all access to those materials. E-books pose similar issues.

Two initiatives are trying to help in this arena: Portico, developed and supported by ITHAKA, and Lots Of Copies Keeps Stuff Safe (LOCKSS), a service based out of Stanford University. Portico provides 'a permanent archive of electronic journals, books, and other scholarly content.'[15] Libraries pay a yearly subscription fee to Portico. In return, if a journal ceases publication, the libraries that paid for subscriptions to that journal will receive electronic access through Portico's dark archive. Libraries can identify titles of journals, e-books, and other scholarly content for Portico to collect.

While Portico is a service, LOCKSS is a tool. It is a free 'open-source, peer-to-peer, decentralized digital preservation infrastructure.'[16] LOCKSS is designed to allow libraries to 'easily and inexpensively collect and preserve their own copies of authorized e-content.'[17] Libraries install the LOCKSS software on an older PC, which is then turned into a 'LOCKSS Box.' Members of participating libraries select titles to be collected and archived. Participating publishers add a permissions page to their websites, which the application then recognizes. Through the administrative interface, librarians from participating institutions can collect and preserve open access publications as well as electronic journals and e-books to which they subscribe. In the event that a journal ceases to exist, libraries with current subscriptions can continue to provide access to members of their community.

Both LOCKSS and Portico are digital preservation initiatives aimed at allowing libraries to access materials to which they subscribe as well as open access journals and other types of freely available scholarship. A third initiative, CLOCKSS (Controlled LOCKSS), is a partnership between libraries and publishers whose mission it is to 'build a sustainable, geographically distributed dark archive with which to ensure the long-term survival of Web-based scholarly publications for the benefit of the greater global research community.' If a trigger event occurs, materials held in CLOCKSS will be freely, publicly available. At this point, there have been three journals that have been discontinued, thereby triggering the public release of their articles.[18] Individuals can freely access materials from these journals from the CLOCKSS website.

Sustaining digital collections

Within digital repositories, it is not enough to focus exclusively on the objects; the repository team should also devote some ongoing effort to supporting collections. With open access repositories of scholarly articles, librarians need to work with faculty on an ongoing basis to sustain momentum and growth in the repository. In libraries with liaisons to academic departments, these librarians can work on ongoing retrospective OA deposit projects – i.e., review faculty CVs, identify articles in journals that publishers will permit to be deposited in a repository, and work with the faculty members or their assistants to deposit the articles. If the library is willing to integrate this type of project into its day-to-day operational work that staff members are held accountable for, it will help to sustain the collection.

Getting a broader group of library staff members involved in ongoing work tied to the repository also helps support the organization as it gradually shifts repository work from being on the fringe into a mode of production for the library as a whole. This new mode of production creates a parallel to how many libraries support their print collections. Instead of having one librarian or department responsible for all aspects of selecting, acquiring, cataloging, and eventually weeding the collection, several individuals are involved in different points in that process. Bringing more people into repository work – even at a slow pace – will ultimately help shift the culture around this new work.

For other types of collections, working with assessment data can lead to projects such as enhancing the metadata, creating new marketing strategies for particular collections, or developing new ways to draw people into the collection. For collections that are tied to the curriculum, experiment by creating records in the library catalog system for some strategically-selected groups of digital objects. As an experiment, review syllabi in a few classes that have large amounts of related materials in repository. For instance, if your repository has a significant amount of images related to classical archaeology and art history, find the corresponding classes in the art history, classics, and archaeology departments. Review the syllabi. Create groups of images as appropriate: 'Etruscans,' 'amphora,' 'Geometric period.' Then create MAchine-Readable Cataloging (MARC) records in the library catalog system with links to the groups in the digital repository. After one semester, review the usage data and decide to expand the groups, work with other classes, or try something else altogether different.

Sustaining repository teams

Like all employees, members of repository teams need to be invested in. Professional development funds have been heavily cut at most institutions. There are many free and inexpensive ways to keep repository team members engaged and learning, but it is important to note that digital repository work is new and continually evolving, and the best way to stay informed of current developments is through attending conferences and meetings. Within this field, research is often presented at conferences before it is published, although the increase in open access journals is speeding up the time between article submission and article publication.

Bringing information in from the outside is useful, but be sure to give the repository team ample opportunities for growth within their existing jobs and within the organization. The nature of project work creates opportunities for different members of the team to take leadership roles and serve as project managers. However, project management work can be challenging for staff without a formal authority, so it is particularly important that all members of the project team are held accountable for their work on the project.

If the repository program is able to hire interns or student workers, have other members of the team besides the program coordinator be their direct supervisor. Management experience can be difficult to get; let staff members gain this experience by managing students.

Grant proposals also present a range of opportunities for professional development. For employees who have not yet been part of a grant proposal or award, have them volunteer to serve as a grant proposal reviewer. Serving as a reviewer is an excellent way to gain exposure to the grant review process and allows staff to get a first-hand view of what makes or breaks a proposal.

For library staff members who are not part of the core repository team, this work can present opportunities for them to grow as well. If staff members are interested, they have available time, and their skills, experience, or aptitude are in line with repository work, project work can be an excellent growth opportunity.

It can be particularly challenging to find the right people to support a repository program. Coordinator roles require a certain amount of understanding of both libraries and technology. Programmers can leave for higher-paying corporate IT jobs. Metadata work takes a specialized set of skills that is difficult to find. While it is unreasonable to expect any employee to stay in a single position for most of his or her career, it is expensive to have a high turnover rate. Invest in employees so that they stay engaged, committed, and energized.

Sustaining the repository program

Ultimately, it is most important to sustain the program itself through support from the library administration. Keep the library's administrative team – and the rest of the library staff – informed of the program's developments and accomplishments. Include members of the administrative team on the repository steering group if possible. Keeping the program closely aligned with the library and university's strategic goals will tremendously help sustain support for the program.

Notes

1. DSpace @ MIT (n.d.). Format support. Retrieved January 20, 2010 from http://libraries.mit.edu/dspace-mit/build/policies/format.html
2. DSpace @ MIT (n.d.). DSpace format reference collection. Retrieved January 20, 2010 from http://libraries.mit.edu/dspace-mit/build/policies/format.html#formats

3. MetaArchive Cooperative (n.d). Collections. Retrieved January 20, 2010 from http://www.metaarchive.org/collections
4. Consultative Committee for Space Data Systems (2002). Reference model for an open archival information system (OAIS). Retrieved on January 20, 2010 from http://public .ccsds.org/publications/archive/650x0b1.pdf
5. PREMIS Editorial Committee (2008). PREMIS data dictionary for preservation metadata. Retrieved on January 20, 2010 from http://www.loc.gov/standards/premis/v2/premis-2-0.pdf
6. Trustworthy repositories audit & certification: Criteria and Checklist (2007) Retrieved on January 20, 2010 from http://www.crl.edu/sites/default/files/attachments/pages/trac_0.pdf
7. National digital information infrastructure and preservation program (n.d.). About the program. Retrieved on January 20, 2010 from http://www.digitalpreservation.gov/library/index .html
8. National digital information infrastructure and preservation program (n.d). Partner tools and services. Retrieved on January 20, 2010 from http://www.digitalpreservation.gov/partners/resources/tools/index.html
9. DigitalPreservationEurope (n.d.). Retrieved on January 20, 2010 from http://www.digitalpreservationeurope.eu/
10. DigitalPreservationEurope YouTube channel (n.d.). Retrieved on January 20, 2010 from http://www.youtube.com/user/wepreserve
11. DigitalPreservationEurope (n.d). The third digital preservation challenge. Retrieved January 20, 2010 from http://www.digitalpreservationeurope.eu/challenge/challenge3/
12. Internet archive (n.d.). Retrieved on January 20, 2010 from http://www.archive.org
13. HTTrack (n.d.). Retrieved on January 20, 2010 from http://httrack.com
14. backupify (n.d.). Retrieved on January 20, 2010 from http://backupify.com
15. Portico (n.d.). Retrieved on January 20, 2010 from http://www.portico.org
16. LOCKSS (n.d.). Retrieved on January 20, 2010 from http://lockss.stanford.edu/lockss/Home
17. Ibid.

18. CLOCKSS (n.d.). Triggered content. Retrieved on January 20, 2010 from http://www.clockss.org/clockss/Triggered_Content. SAGE Publications discontinued its journals *Graft: Organ and Cell Transplantation* and *Auto/Biography*. Oxford University Press discontinued its journal *Brief Treatment and Crisis Intervention*. Materials from these publications are now freely available through the CLOCKSS website.

10

Assessment

Introduction

Assessment, or the process of gathering data to use for purposes of evaluation and making decisions, is an important (and yet often overlooked) area for program developers and project managers. Assessment is the method of measuring performance against clearly stated, defined goals and objectives. It is the iterative process of setting goals, gathering data, analyzing results, evaluating performance, and then recalibrating accordingly.

Assessment for digital repositories needs to occur at various points: at the program level (is the program achieving its goals? Are services meeting users' needs?), the collection level (is this particular collection meeting its goals?), and the systems or interface level (are users able to find what they're looking for? Is the system able to support most projects? Does it provide the functionality needed?)

The high-level process for analyzing the performance of individuals, programs, services, and collections is the same, but each raises different questions or areas to focus on and might require different methods of data collection.

Guiding principles

Set useful, realistic goals and stick to them.
Set SMART goals: Specific, Measurable, Attainable, Relevant, and Time-bound.

Make sure that the goals are possible to achieve within your environment. You can always increase your goals and expectations, but don't aim too high, especially when starting a new program.

Don't wait to make changes in processes and policies if changes are necessary.
Make incremental changes and tweak processes to improve them on an ongoing basis.

Perform full-scale assessments on a regular basis; define those timeframes in advance.
Determine what the appropriate timeframe is for different types of assessment and follow through. For example, collect feedback from faculty by sending out a web survey once a year. Compare data from each year's survey. Perform a full-scale assessment of systems every three years. For collections, work with content owners to craft questions you plan to answer through assessment; follow up six months later.

Make decisions based on data.
Use data to guide the decision-making process and ongoing strategic planning.

Don't be scared of potential results.
Learn how to translate data – even negative reviews – into something constructive and meaningful.

Overview of the process

Start by writing goals and objectives. What is it that you are trying to accomplish? How? By what date? Use these questions plus the goals and objectives for the repository program, the library, and the institution itself. Not all of the goals and objectives for a repository program should be accomplished in a given year, so create objectives for the upcoming year. Collections, services, and individuals should also have their own goals and objectives as well.

The difference between goals and objectives is that goals are broad and vague – the overarching themes – while objectives are specific and measurable. Goals should be aligned with a library's or institution's strategic plan; objectives are the methods by which you achieve those goals. Some examples of typical university library goals:

- Goal 1: Support faculty research and scholarship.
- Goal 2: Support excellence in teaching and learning.
- Goal 3: Provide tools to support access to information in digital and analog formats.

Objectives, which ideally should each be tied to a goal, are more explicit and precise. A sample objective for the repository program's strategic plan, one that could be tied to 'Goal 1: Support faculty research and scholarship,' might be: 'Develop open access repositories to make faculty scholarship more accessible.'

One way to think about developing objectives is through the mnemonic device, 'SMART' – create objectives that are Specific, Measurable, Attainable, Realistic, and Time-Bound. This criteria is applicable for developing objectives for individuals, programs, and collections. Furthermore, explicitly align objectives to departmental and library-wide goals. It helps employees to understand how their yearly objectives and the department's work coincide with the work of the department and the library as a whole. Include this information in formal performance planning documents and reviews if possible.

After a pre-determined amount of time has elapsed, data must be collected to determine if objectives have been met. Typical data collection methods include: surveys, focus groups, usability studies, and through system or website logs. A combination of quantitative data and qualitative information should be used as the basis for analysis. Quantitative data is numeric and is gathered from large samples. Qualitative data is the reverse – it is data gathered to try to understand human behavior. It is gathered through focus groups, descriptive answers to questions, and watching how users navigate websites. Both types of research have a place in digital repository assessment. See Figure 10.1, 'Quantitative and qualitative data,' for examples of instruments to gather each type of data.

Surveys often use Likert items when crafting questions. A typical five-value Likert item question would include the following answers:

- Strongly agree
- Agree
- Neutral (neither agree nor disagree)
- Disagree
- Strongly disagree

Figure 10.1 Quantitative and qualitative data

Quantitative data	Surveys, log analysis data, website statistics
Qualitative data	Focus groups, user group discussions, long-form answers to questions in surveys

194

These responses are then coded on a 5 to 1 scale: 'strongly agree' responses are given a score of 5, 'agree' responses are given a score of 4, and so on. The data is then represented on a scale.

Once the data has been collected, analyze the results. Look for patterns and trends, but also look for aberrations. For quantitative data, look at the mean and median responses to questions. Create graphs for answers to key questions. For qualitative data, highlight representative quotes and identify trends. Compile lists of recommendations and suggestions. Identify areas for improvement in the future. Try to determine possible reasons for the success and underperformance of collections or services. Put all of this information – graphs, charts, results, and a written narrative – together into a year-end report for the repository program.

Assessing the repository program and its services

Assessment needs to occur on multiple levels: assessing the program as a whole and the services it offers, individual collections, and also the performance of individuals. Individuals' performance should occur as part of a library-, IT-, or university-wide review process and should follow the same standardized procedures and criteria for evaluation used for all employees. The focus here is on assessment for the repository program, its services, and individual collections. At the highest level, the program itself should be evaluated. First, gather feedback from users. Is the program meeting the needs of its users? Is it meeting the needs that it was set out to accomplish? What areas could be improved? In what areas is it most successful?

What services are most highly rated? What services are being taken advantage of most frequently? How do members of each constituency (faculty, staff, students, alumni, etc.) feel about the technical support they receive in using various systems? See Figure 10.2, 'Questions to consider,' for additional ideas to build into assessment questions.

Gathering feedback from content owners

The repository team should make a concerted effort to gather feedback from content owners/collection liaisons on a regular basis, at least once a year. For new partners, gathering feedback on a regular basis is part of the process to transition from building a collection to sustaining a collection. For pre-existing collections, it is important to maintain communication on a regular basis. Any type of communication is an opportunity for the repository team to remind the content owner that they are providing a regular, ongoing service; that the collection is still in existence; and may trigger ideas for improvement or adding to the collection. It is worth the investment of time to check in with content owners on a yearly basis, either through

Figure 10.2 Questions to consider

Do students know how to access collections? Do they know what collections exist? Do they know what services the department offers? Which services are most important to them? What additional services would they use? Is feedback collected after instructional sessions/workshops?

Do faculty members know how to submit proposals? Do they have adequate support from the repository team to submit a proposal?

For faculty members who have submitted project proposals, how satisfied were they with the proposal process? Was enough information conveyed?

an informal conversation or through a more formal process of gathering data such as a survey. For institutions with a limited number of collections, take the time to make the personal connection and have an in-person conversation or phone call with content owners.

Auditing the repository

Gathering feedback from users is only one aspect of assessing the program. In addition to learning what users think about the program and its services, repository teams need to do self-assessments as well, ideally measuring their infrastructure, programs, services, plans, and repositories against current best practices and benchmarks. Self-assessments should highlight what the repository team thinks its strengths are but also identify areas for improvement.

The Digital Curation Centre (DCC) and Digital PreservationEurope have put together a toolkit designed to facilitate this process and allow coordinators to evaluate their own repositories.[1] This toolkit, the Digital Repository Audit Method Based on Risk Assessment (DRAMBORA), is available in two formats: an interactive version available from the DRAMBORA website and a downloadable packet including background information, templates, and spreadsheets. While the toolkit was designed for large repositories, it can easily be adapted to smaller repositories and can serve as the framework for internal audits.

Collection-level usage data

In addition to looking at the program as a whole, repository managers must evaluate the performance of individual collections. Are collections performing up to expectations? If not, why not? How does collection usage compare between collections? How does usage compare between this year and past years?

Collecting usage data will allow you to better understand how users are accessing the collections, their search strategies, search behaviors, and what they were looking for – whether or not they found it. Many repository systems come with tools to collect usage data, but these tools are not always adequate for reporting purposes. If the repository's log analysis tool is insufficient and the system uses a relational database, a programmer could write a tool that will allow repository managers to construct queries or reports to extract meaningful data. As a minimum, you need to be able to see counts and lists of access and searches, by collection and across all collections.

Data also needs to be able to be extracted by users or types of users. It is important to make a distinction between the needs and behavior of core constituents (faculty, staff, students, and any other groups identified in the strategic plan such as alumni) and the general public. For publicly accessible collections that do not require individual logins, it will not be possible to get a pure separation of usage by institutional users versus non-institutional users. But you can make some reasonable assumptions based on geographic location. One of the specifications for the log analysis tool should be to separate on-campus usage versus off-campus usage. However, between students and faculty who live off campus and the increase in wireless availability, this separation may be misleading. It is worth going one step further and isolating local users (if possible) as well. If you include a script to look up IP addresses as part of the process, it will simplify the amount of human time needed to cull through results.

The two areas to focus on are access and queries. Who is using your collections? Which collections? How are they being used? Are the same individuals repeated users? How are users finding the collections? What page is their launch pad? Once in a collection, approximately how many searches do individuals do? Do they look at thumbnails or download high-resolution images? For articles, are users reading abstracts or downloading the full-text version of articles? In terms of queries, what kinds of search terms are users looking for? Are they finding what they were looking for? If not, why? Does the repository include items that should have been in the results returned? Is metadata insufficient? Are items not being full-text indexed? Is the object outside of the scope of what is being collected? Or is this an opportunity to grow the collection? Here is where it is important to note whether users are part of the core constituencies or not. While it is helpful to look at search queries to make collection development decisions, it is important to know if these queries were from core constituencies or not. Do not make collection development decisions based on the needs of the public unless this is part of your program's strategic direction. See Figures 10.3, 'Access log' and Figure 10.4, 'Query log' for examples of access logs and query logs.

Looking at usage data can also uncover some unexpected ways in which people are using collections and can lead to ongoing metadata projects. For example, if users are searching by keyword for 'food' and 'apples' and getting zero results, consider adding broader keywords to items with more specific terms – 'fruit.' For biology-related collections, this might mean adding common names to genus and species, i.e., adding 'bees,' 'honeybees,' and 'honey bees' to all items with the subject '*Apis mellifera.*'

Some of this data should be shared with content owners and collection liaisons on a regular basis – either monthly or

Figure 10.3 Access log

date	time	event	source_ip	user	action	collection_name	id
1/2/2010	20:41:51	access	128.195.178.209	ucuser	login successful	World War I Photos	56034
1/2/2010	20:42:40	access	128.195.178.209	ucuser	logout	World War I Photos	56035
1/3/2010	20:36:22	access	128.195.162.33	ucuser	login successful	World War I Photos	56255
1/3/2010	20:54:19	access	128.195.162.33	ucuser	logout	World War I Photos	56256

Figure 10.4 Query log

Subject Equals apis mellifera
Subject Equals pollen
KEYWORDS honey
KEYWORDS honeybee
KEYWORDS bees
KEYWORDS fruit
KEYWORDS apple
KEYWORDS pear
KEYWORDS banana
KEYWORDS bananas
Artist Equals Cezanne
KEYWORDS Cezanne
KEYWORDS gold
KEYWORDS marriage
KEYWORDS women
KEYWORDS woman
KEYWORDS snow
Subject Equals Construction and Plans

yearly, depending upon the needs of the individuals or collections. Many departments write end-of-year reports, and this data can be important documentation. If departments need to access the data more frequently, send automated reports on a pre-determined basis or create a method for individuals to access data for their collections on their own.

Website statistics

While different than usage logs associated with repository systems, website statistics are also valuable. Google Analytics[2] is free and can be used with any website for which you control the domain. Many colleges and universities are already using Google Analytics to monitor traffic on their websites. It may be necessary to work with the domain administrator to access data for the library or repository team's specific web pages.

Statcounter[3] is another tool to monitor website traffic. Statcounter offers free accounts to monitor the most recent 500 page loads on your website. Low-cost paid accounts will track more page loads and visitors. With Statcounter, you can see how individual users got to your site, track their usage through your site, see how long they are on any given page, and see returning visits. It is a useful tool for gathering data to determine how visitors are moving through your web pages.

Conclusion

The data itself that is compiled is important for reporting, but what is truly valuable is what you do with that data. Use the data gathered through surveys, conversations with key constituents, usage statistics, and web traffic to better understand how individuals are using collections and how they feel about services being provided. Make changes to the program based on this data. What are the strengths of the collection? What are areas to build upon? What areas need to be strengthened? How can marketing plans be improved based on feedback from users? Should metadata be enhanced? How can collection development efforts be improved based on users' search queries? Should policies, processes, or priorities be changed based on trends in data? Don't be afraid of the results; use data as the springboard for improving performance and user satisfaction.

Notes

1. DRAMBORA interactive (n.d.) Retrieved on January 17, 2010 from http://www.repositoryaudit.eu/
2. Google analytics (n.d.). Retrieved on January 17, 2010 from http://www.google.com/analytics
3. Statcounter (n.d.). Retrieved on January 17, 2010 from http://www.statcounter.com

11

Web 2.0 and digital repositories

Introduction

In the mid-2000s, a noticeable shift began to emerge among the most popular websites, a shift that is commonly referred to as 'Web 2.0.' Web 2.0 is not a specific thing, but rather it is a set of characteristics that form the basis for a dramatic change in how users interact with the Internet, websites, and each other. Some of the key characteristics that are related to repository work include making websites more interactive and user-centered; encouraging user-created content; and allowing for data to be extracted from one system and imported and used elsewhere, for different purposes.

Guiding principles

Use Web 2.0 tools and services to push repository content out from the library.
Take content to where your users are – and where other users might stumble upon the repository content. Use tools to allow users to view and manipulate content in new ways. The repository should be the digital archive for content, but it does not have to be the one and only home for it.

Pay attention to changes in technology and user behavior.
Keep your systems and services current. Investigate new tools as they are developed. Plug-ins can keep systems and services fresh and interesting.

Create opportunities to encourage user participation.
Even if your system is not designed to allow users to comment on objects or make recommendations, create ways to get the campus community involved in the repository.

Push content out; bring users in

Instead of relying on users to come to the repository, look for ways to push content out – into other systems and through referrals. Many libraries and archives are uploading images from their collections to Flickr – both historical images and recent, current photos of the campus. Cornell University, Georgia State University, Loughborough University, North Carolina State University, University of Maryland Baltimore County, and the University of Tulsa are just a few of the academic libraries with a presence in Flickr.[1]

The Library of Congress launched a pilot project in January 2008 to post images to Flickr. In October 2008, they issued a report documenting their experiences, *For the common good: The Library of Congress Flickr pilot project* and an accompanying summary report.[2] The Library received a great deal of public support for the project, and it is considered to be a great success. 'The Flickr project increases awareness of the Library and its collections; sparks creative interaction with collections; provides LC staff with experience with social tagging and Web 2.0 community input; and allows the Library to provide leadership to cultural heritage and government communities.'[3]

While most academic libraries are not trying to provide leadership to cultural heritage and government communities, the rest of the results would be applicable for other libraries considering contributing content to Flickr. Since the pilot's launch, the Library has continued to add materials to the site on a weekly basis. Uploading content to Flickr is easy, and it is free for the first 100 mb per month. For institutions uploading large amounts of content, upgrading to the Pro version costs $24.95/year.[4] It is a low-cost, low-barrier way to get the library involved in Web 2.0.

By using Wikipedia, repository teams can create several opportunities to drive users to their collections.[5] Write an entry for your publicly available collections. Add links to your collections from the growing list of digital library projects.[6] From within relevant entries, add links to your collections. If your library has its own entry, add links there as well. For public domain images, libraries might want to consider uploading photos to Wikimedia Commons, a database of 'freely usable media files to which anyone can contribute.'[7]

Within the institution, push content into the course management system or an institutional portal. Librarians can work with faculty to embed links to groups of objects from the repository into BlackBoard or any other course management system. Create an 'image of the day' feature to embed content into a portal system or post on the library or institution's website.

Digital video benefits from being embedded into web pages. While the repository should house archival-quality footage, provide users with other (better) ways to view video. Consider streaming video from an off-site host and embedding the footage into a browser, similar to what users have come to expect from YouTube. See Chapter 3, 'Technical infrastructure' for more details.

In general, work to push content to where your users are; don't make users work to get to your repository system and content.

Integrate Web 2.0 tools with the repository

By taking advantage of interesting new tools being developed outside of the digital library world, you have the ability to extend the capabilities of repository systems and keep the look and feel of collections' websites fresh. CoolIris,[8] a web browser plugin, can be integrated into any website or repository using the Media RSS standard. Website developers can use CoolIris to create groups of images and display them in an elegant slide show. Users who opt to install the CoolIris plugin can view images and video on a 3D wall.

CoolIris is a small, simple example of a way to take advantage of outside technology to update a repository interface or website. For institutions with programming resources, it is possible to push the boundaries of the repository much further. The Islandora Project,[9] created at the University of Prince Edward Island, 'combines the Drupal and Fedora software applications to create a robust digital asset management system that can be used for any requirement where collaboration and digital data stewardship, for the short and long term, are critical.' Drupal,[10] a content management system, can be directly integrated with Fedora, which extends the functionality of both systems and opens up tremendous possibilities for the repository. Several plug-ins such as the KML Module[11] have been developed for Drupal so users can access GIS data (and specifically, Google Earth content) through Drupal. The KML Module will 'determine order of nodes that are displayed in Google Earth, allowing for alphabetical or time-based flythroughs of nodes.'[12] By integrating several of these systems, developers can build web-based projects pulling images from a Fedora repository, using functionality from Google Earth, and offering a Drupal front-end.

These are just a few examples of ways to extend the functionality of a repository system. Open source projects, rapid development time, and an increased interest in development within the library/information science community are all creating new opportunities. The bottom line is that repository systems do not need to end with an out-of-the-box installation with minimal customizations. Particularly if you are using open source systems, the possibilities are limited only by your imagination.

However, there are some risks associated with both open source systems and creating bridges between systems. Some open source applications are updated often, which requires some upkeep for systems/applications administrators. Every time source code is updated, you run the risk of having your code break. Open source communities do collapse, and there is no guarantee that your software will continue to be supported. Realistically, proprietary software runs the same risks: companies are often bought and sold, companies stop supporting particular systems, and any customized code written for your particular system might not work with an update in the future.

User participation

User participation is one of the defining characteristics of Web 2.0. While most repository systems do not come with out-of-the-box functionality to support user-contributed content, you can build such functionality into a system or take the spirit of Web 2.0 and find alternate ways to encourage user participation without doing it in the repository system itself. Look for ways to allow users the opportunity to interact with digital objects; make 'user engagement' a goal for the repository program.

Consider adopting functionality that allows users to 'tag' digital objects, submit comments, make recommendations, create and save groups, and create slideshows. Folksonomies, or the compilation of user-created tags for digital objects in a particular collection, are becoming particularly widespread and can lead to some interesting opportunities for metadata work.

Alternatively, find ways to engage your community outside of the repository itself. Propose ideas to faculty to encourage them to have students build collections as an assignment. See Chapter 7, 'Content recruitment and marketing,' for suggested ways to have members of the institution build collections.

Notes

1. Flickr (n.d.). Retrieved on January 21, 2010 from http://www .flickr.com
2. Springer, M., Dulabahn, B., Michel, P., Natanson, B., Reser, D., Woodward, D., et al. (2008). *For the common good: The Library of Congress Flickr pilot project.* Washington, DC: Library of Congress. Retrieved on January 21, 2010 from http://www.loc.gov/rr/print/flickr_report_final.pdf
3. Springer, M., Dulabahn, B., Michel, P., Natanson, B., Reser, D., Woodward, D., et al. (2008). *For the common good: The Library of Congress Flickr pilot project, report summary* (p. 6). Washington, DC: Library of Congress. Retrieved on January 21, 2010 from http://www.loc.gov/rr/print/flickr_ report_final_summary.pdf
4. Flickr (n.d.) *Free accounts, upgrading, and gifts.* Retrieved on January 30, 2010 from http://www.flickr.com/help/limits/
5. Lally, A. M., Dunford, C.E. (2007). Using Wikipedia to extend digital collections. *D-Lib Magazine,* **13**(5/6), May/June.

Retrieved on January 21, 2010 from http://www.dlib.org/dlib/may07/lally/05lally.html

6. Wikipedia (n.d.). *List of digital library projects.* Retrieved on January 21, 2010 from http://en.wikipedia.org/wiki/List_of_digital_library_projects

7. Wikimedia Commons (n.d.). Retrieved on January 21, 2010 from http://commons.wikimedia.org/wiki/Main_Page

8. CoolIris (n.d.). Retrieved on January 22, 2010 from http://www.cooliris.com

9. Islandora project (n.d.). Retrieved on January 22, 2010 from http://www.islandora.ca

10. Drupal (n.d.). Retrieved on January 22, 2010 from http://www.drupal.org

11. Drupal (n.d.). *KML module.* Retrieved on January 22, 2010 from http://drupal.org/project/kml

12. Ibid.

Concluding thoughts

As you move forward to build or sustain a digital repository program, keep some guiding principles in mind:

Fit the program to the institution.
No two institutions are the same – and no two repository programs should be identical as a result. Focus on the environment, technical infrastructure, staffing, budget, and culture for your institution. Build a program in response to the needs of that particular institution at that point in time.

A repository program is not a static entity – it should evolve over time.
Users' needs, institutional goals, and technology all change. The repository program, its services and systems, should all reflect those changes. Incorporate changes in technology into the repository – for example, shifting to cloud-based storage, working with virtual servers, and allowing users to contribute their own content. Stay current.

It's about the university, not the library.
Content should be collected from around the university, not only from library collections. In order to gain momentum, you will need to garner interest from elsewhere within the institution, and you will need to demonstrate that the repository is truly there to support the needs of the university as a whole. If you start by creating library-related collections,

it will be challenging to get others particularly interested. Start with non-library collections, gain a critical mass of content, and then begin to work with library-owned materials.

Maintaining support from the library's administration is critically important.
While the focus of the repository should be on the institution as a whole, the library's administration plays a pivotal role as they will ultimately decide whether or not to continue a program. Don't work on creating a repository program without solid support. If your staff promises faculty members that their scholarship or other digital objects will be accessible and usable in a few years, the library needs to be prepared to follow through on that promise.

Keep thinking about the big picture.
How do these systems and services work together? What are the major challenges for the near future and longer-term future? What can the repository team do to be prepared? What challenges is the institution facing and can a repository support any of these challenges?

Use time wisely.
Allow yourself ample time to invest in planning: strategic planning for the program; project planning at the collection-level; planning for the future. Recognize that jumping into a task head first is not necessarily the best way to handle a new situation. Think about the workflow, consider various ways to handle the work, try one approach, and refine it. It is often far more cost-effective to invest time to work with a programmer to write a script to automate routine tasks rather than taking up valuable staff time to do work a program can do for you. At the end of a project or a milestone, take time to document the experience, decisions made, and

recommendations for the future. Don't wait until you have time in the future – those opportunities rarely occur.

What's next?

In the early 2000s, several issues tied to intellectual property laws and regulations have come to a very public breaking point. Peer-to-peer (P2P) file sharing using protocols such as BitTorrent make it possible to share large files, which have led to the rise of torrent hosting sites such as The Pirate Bay. Many of the files hosted on such sites include copyrighted material, thus raising the ire of the music and movie industries and leading to some very public debates regarding copyright restrictions.

Digital video has become far easier to shoot and edit over the past few years. More students are creating videos as part of their course work; to advertise or support co-curricular activities such as fraternities and sororities, teams, or other group activities; or just for fun as artistic expression. Most students have a natural inclination to add a music track to their videos. Very quickly, students move from working within fair use exceptions to being in the fuzzy gray area and then to outside of that protection. Whose responsibility is it if copyrighted music is embedded into a video that is deposited into a digital repository? Does it matter? What if the video was part of a service learning project and a non-profit is now hosting that student's work on their website?

Lawrence Lessig, in his 2007 TED Talk, said:

> We have to recognize [our kids] are different from us. We made mixed tapes, they remix music. We watched TV, they make TV. It is technology that has made them different. And as we see what this technology can do,

we need to recognize that you can't kill the instinct the technology produces, we can only criminalize it. We can't stop our kids from using it, we can only drive it underground. We can't make our kids passive again, we can only make them 'pirates.' And is that good?[1]

Regardless of how we feel about these rules, while working within an academic community it is particularly important that we understand what the guidelines are – and educate our students about them. This does not mean that we can't actively work to support change in copyright laws, but we also should be working to educate students about existing legislation and guidelines.

At the other end of the spectrum, repository work also entails working with faculty and other authors who are concerned about their intellectual property – their scholarship – being appropriated by others, particularly if their articles are deposited in a repository. While that idea or paragraph or article can easily be plagiarized if it is published in a printed journal, many scholars fear the ease with which articles can be read and downloaded. The repository team needs to be prepared to handle this range of questions and concerns.

In conclusion

Building a repository program can take a tremendous amount of work, energy, and time. But it can also be particularly rewarding to see the collection you created being used by faculty, students, and staff. Repository work is a continuation of traditional library work, but it takes the library out of the library building. Our work is no longer tied to the library building. It's not about the collections housed under the library's roof. Instead, it's about becoming embedded and involved in the information lifecycle within the institution – supporting faculty, staff, and students creating new forms of information and digital objects; collecting, describing, organizing, and curating these objects; disseminating them within the broader digital landscape; and preserving them throughout their lifecycle. The work is fundamentally the same, but the digital environment has broadly expanded who can create new forms of information; how that information is created; the scale, scope, and quantity of information created; and the complexity of issues tied to sustaining a digital object over time. Once books go on a library shelf, they require minimal work to be maintained. Digital objects, on the other hand, require continued work. Launching a collection is just one phase in a digital object's lifespan.

Furthermore, digital repository work gives us an opportunity to act as change agents in support of development, progress using digital technology, new forms of scholarship and scholarly discourse. We can serve as advocates to try to convince the academy as a whole that digital scholarship should count towards tenure. Libraries can stop taking a generally conservative approach when it comes to copyright and fair use. We are in a position to push the boundaries and try to improve the situation for the next generation, those who are creating new digital content and remixing existing content into new forms of media.

We need to listen to our core groups of users – mainly, students and faculty – and consider their research habits and workflows, how they create digital objects and information, how they *really* work, not just how they *think* they work – so we can develop appropriate tools to support them. This is a time of excitement and energy in the library world; we need to embrace the changes. We need to be flexible, nimble, and agile – support changes in our users and in technology, and be prepared for the future.

Note

1. Lessig, L. (2007). *Larry Lessig on laws that choke creativity.* TED. Retrieved on January 31, 2010 from http://www.ted. com/talks/larry_lessig_says_the_law_is_strangling_creativity. html

Appendix 1:
Introduction to
metadata workshop

The metadata workshop was originally designed as a series of exercises to teach technical services support staff about metadata, but it has been adapted to teach IT staff, chief information officers (CIOs), and also public service librarians the basics about metadata. It is a quick way to understand some of the challenges of working with a range of digital objects, the varying types of information that need to be conveyed, and the lack of authoritative information available about most digital objects. The workshop as described below is an abbreviated version, designed to last for one session (1.5 to 2 hours). It works well as an exercise to introduce the library staff as a whole or library/IT staff to digital repository work.

Purpose

For participants to learn the basics of metadata production

For technical services staff: understand how the work of metadata differs from traditional cataloging. Specifically:

- Within digital repositories, there are multiple metadata standards and no 'one size fits all' standard in the way that all library catalogs use MARC and data is described using AACR2.

■ For digital objects, there is often no thesaurus to use to assign subject terms.

■ For digital objects, there is often no authoritative source of information about the object.

For public services staff: gain a basic understanding of the type of work that goes into metadata production. Become familiar with Dublin Core and other metadata standards used in the course of the workshop. Gain exposure to working with thesauri and crosswalks. Through the experience, individuals can learn if this is work they are interested in assisting with.

For information technology staff: gain a basic understanding of the type of work that goes into metadata production.

For library and technology administrators: understand the complexity of the work needed to create metadata for an entire collection.

Materials

Sample digital objects (adapt as necessary to represent collections at your institution, representing as much variety as possible):

■ Scanned art slides – licensed from vendors.

■ A unique digital object, a digital image from a faculty collection or research center, ideally something unusual. Example: photograph of a construction site from a civil engineering collection.

■ A digital photograph of a three-dimensional object from the university, something tied to coursework. Example: World War II posters used in a history course.

- An article written by a faculty member – either a pre-print or post-print.

Four objects per team. One packet per object which includes:

- A printed copy of the digital object.
- A written note about the collection, its intended purpose, and audience.
- Any available data associated with the object – notes from the vendor, transcription of information written on the back of a photograph, information from the content owner, whatever is available.

Metadata schema handouts:

- Printed handouts with Dublin Core fields – 2 per team per object.
- Printed handouts with VRA Core fields – 2 per team per object.
- Printed handouts with MARC fields – 2 per team per object.
- Printed handouts with any other standards used – 2 per team per object.
- Printed grid used to create hybrid standards – 2 per team per object.

If teams have access to computers: website set up in advance with links to each standard and explanations about associated fields. Include links to any thesauri that could be relevant.

If teams do not have access to computers: printed copies of each standard and explanation of its associated fields, one copy per team. Include links to any thesauri that could be relevant.

List of potentially relevant subject thesauri:

- Getty Union List of Authors' Names (ULAN), Art & Architecture Thesaurus (AAT), Thesaurus of Geographic Names (TGN).

- Library of Congress Subject Headings (LCSH), Thesaurus for Graphic Materials (TGM); Medical Subject Headings (MeSH).

- Special Libraries Association – News Division's Keywords for News.

Handout (one per team per collection/object):

Questions to consider
Collection: _____
What worked well with MARC? What didn't?
What worked well with Dublin Core? What didn't?
What worked well with VRA Core? What didn't?
What controlled vocabulary did you choose to use? Notes about using a thesaurus for this collection.
Notes about your ideal standard for this collection.

Procedures

1. Introduce the project. Have participants break up into small groups – either pairs or groups of three to four people. If participants come from different backgrounds (technical services, public services, IT), have them split up so they have at least one person from each group per team.

2. Hand out the first packet with printouts of digital objects and associated data to each team. Also distribute metadata schema handouts to each team. Have participants work with the schemas in this order: MARC, Dublin Core,

VRA Core, create a new or hybrid collection. Ask teams to try to create metadata for the object according to each schema and answer questions about each scheme.

3. After participants are finished with the first object, facilitate a discussion with all participants. Compare the differences in data each group created. Discuss formatting: how to structure data so it is consistent from one metadata creator to another, one collection to another. Did teams use the same thesaurus? Why or why not?

4. Proceed with the rest of the digital objects, adding an additional task for the second, third, and fourth collections: creating a data dictionary for the schema the team creates.

5. After the teams have finished working on all of the objects, facilitate another discussion as a group. What were the groups' observations? Frustrations? What worked well? What did not?

Instructor's notes

If digital objects are not available from the institution, use sample objects from existing public collections. Ideally, select objects that are representative of collections that you might eventually build. The goal is to have participants work with objects that are as varied and as different from books as possible, objects that represent the range and scope of the metadata work that occurs in a given repository.

If the group of participants does not include anyone familiar with traditional cataloging or MARC, it is not necessary to include MARC for any of the objects. Catalogers coming from a traditional technical services background often have a difficult time understanding why MARC and AACR2 do not lend themselves to digital repository work until they try to work with some more unusual objects.

Appendix 2: The World War II Poster Project

Overview of the project

In an effort to find creative ways to develop students' research, information literacy, and technology skills within the context of a course, David Del Testa (Assistant Professor of History, Bucknell University) and Abby Clobridge (then Librarian and Digital Initiatives Group Leader, Bucknell University) developed the World War II Poster Project, a six-week learning module embedded in an introductory history course, History 100: Thinking about History, the focus of which for this iteration was 'World War II.' Throughout the Poster Project unit, students worked hands-on with original World War II-era posters from the University's archives to enable them to become proficient at the process of describing, researching, analyzing, digitizing, and cataloging the posters, and carry those skills forward to the rest of their college careers.

For the culmination of this project, students wrote papers and built a small, publicly available repository of digital images of the posters and notes about their research. The best student papers were included in the digital repository. The World War II Poster Project has led to the development of two distinct pedagogical models both of which can be (and are being) adapted by library staff at other institutions, independent of the posters themselves.

The first model is one of intense collaboration between faculty with librarians, archivists, and instructional technologists. In the History 100 module, students worked together in pairs under the guidance of an instructional team. The team included librarians, instructional technologists, and archives staff. One of the major objectives of the unit was to expose students to the array of library and technology services and tools to which they now have access, along with introducing them to specific members of the library/technology staff to whom they could turn for assistance at any point during their enrollment at Bucknell. Furthermore, one of the purposes of the intense collaboration was to have students see the teaching and library staff as professional equals, serving different roles in students' learning.

The second pedagogical practice developed by Del Testa and Clobridge through this project is the 'pixels and paper' model. In this model, students create linkages between digital media and physical artifacts by working with a mix of 'analog' sources and 'digital' technologies. Learning modules are structured around this hybrid of analog and digital to encourage good historical practice and analysis. This praxis could be applied to any object (physical or digital), as long as it is 'real' and can serve as the basis of academic scholarship. For instance, a set of political cartoons which could work in a political science or history class; election buttons or posters; postcards or objects from various locations and periods of history.

The richness of the World War II Poster Project in particular comes from a holistic approach for the students: their experiences linking the material and digital worlds; the relationships they created between their individual work and that of the group; and finally, their experiences creating knowledge as professionals.

From 2006 to 2008, Del Testa and Clobridge developed the project, implemented it twice in the classroom, and, most importantly, shifted from the developmental/experimental phase into a fully reproducible model of praxis. At this point, the project has become self-sustaining, and can be implemented regardless of actual personnel deployed or the objects studied. Thus, the project itself has evolved into a model – a template for collaboration, active learning, and object-based learning.

More information about the project, copies of past presentations, and additional resources are all available at http://www.paperandpixels.org and in Chapter 3, 'The World War II Poster Project: Building a Digital Library through Information Literacy Partnerships,' in *Using Technology to Teach Information Literacy*, ed. by Thomas P. Mackey and Trudi E. Jacobson.[1]

Note

1. Clobridge, A. and Del Testa, D. 2008. The World War II poster project: Building a digital library through information literacy partnerships. In T. Mackey & T. Jacobson (Eds.), *Using technology to teach information literacy* (pp. 51–82). New York: Neal-Schuman Publishers.

Bibliography

Art & architecture thesaurus online. (n.d.). Retrieved January 30, 2010 from *http://www.getty.edu/research/ conducting_research/vocabularies/aat/*

Babinec, M. and Mercer, H. (2009). Introduction: Metadata and open access repositories. *Cataloging & Classification Quaterly*, 47(3), 209–211.

Baca, M., Harpring, P., Ward J., & Beecroft, A. (Eds.) (n.d.). Metadata standards crosswalk. Retrieved January 30, 2010 from *http://www.getty.edu/research/conducting_ research/standards/intrometadata/crosswalks.html*

Bailey, C.W. Jr. (2009) Institutional repository bibliography. Retrieved January 30, 2010 from *http://www.digital-scholarship.org/irb/metadata.htm*

BCR's CDP Digital Imaging Best Practices Version 2.0 (2008). Retrieved January 31, 2010 from *http://www.bcr .org/dps/cdp/best/digital-imaging-bp.pdf*

Caplan, P. (2003). *Metadata fundamentals for all librarians.* Chicago, IL: American Library Association.

Clobridge, A. (2008). Starting an institutional repository program in two months or less: The good, the bad, and the ugly. Project briefing: Spring 2008 task force meeting. Retrieved January 5, 2010 from *http://www.cni.org/ tfms/2008a.spring/abstracts/PB-starting-clobridge.html*

Consultative Committee for Space Data Systems (2002). Reference model for an open archival information system (OAIS). Retrieved on January 20, 2010 from *http://public .ccsds.org/publications/archive/650x0b1.pdf*

Crow, R. (2004). A guide to institutional repository software. New York: Open Society Institute. Retrieved January 31, 2010 from *http://www.soros.org/openaccess/pdf/OSI_Guide_to_Institutional_Repository_Software_v2.pdf*

Dahl, M., Banerjee K., & Spalti, M. (2006). *Digital libraries: Integrating content and systems.* London: Chandos Publishing.

Dublin Core metadata best practices, version 2.1.1. (2006) Retrieved January 31, 2010 from *http://www.bcr.org/dps/cdp/best/dublin-core-bp.pdf*

Ferreira, M., Baptista, A., Rodrigues, E., and Saraiva, R. (2008) Carrots and sticks: Some ideas on how to create a successful institutional repository. *D-Lib Magazine,* 14(12). Retrieved on December 19, 2009 from *http://www.dlib.org/dlib/january08/ferreira/01ferreira.html*

Foster, N.F. & Gibbons, S. (2005). Understanding Faculty to Improve Content Recruitment for Institutional Repositories. *D-Lib Magazine,* 11:1. Retrieved January 27, 2010 from *http://www.dlib.org/dlib/january05/foster/01foster.html*

Ganapati, P. (2009). DIY book scanners turn your books into bytes. *Wired.* Retrieved January 30, 2010 from *http://www.wired.com/gadgetlab/2009/12/diy-book-scanner/*

Gieseckie, J. (2008). NIH public access policy: Campus implementation strategies. *Proceedings of the 152nd ARL Membership Meeting.* Retrieved on January 22, 2010 from *http://www.arl.org/resources/pubs/mmproceedings/152mm-proceedings.shtml*

Gueguen, G. (2009). Featured collection: Joyner Library digital collections. *D-Lib Magazine,* 15(7–8). Retrieved January 5, 2010 from *http://www.dlib.org/dlib/july09/07featured-collection.html*

Harnad, S., Brody, T., Vallieres, F., Carr, L., Hitchcock, S., Gingras, Y., et al. (2004). The access/impact problem and the green and gold roads to open access. *Serials Review,*

30(4). Retrieved on January 18, 2010 from *http://eprints .ecs.soton.ac.uk/10209*

Harper, G. (n.d.) University of Texas Copyright Crash Course. Retrieved January 31, 2010 from *http://www. utsystem.edu/ogc/intellectualproperty/cprtindx.htm*

Jacobs, N., Thomas, A., and McGregor, A. (2008) Institutional repositories in the UK: The JISC approach. *Library Trends*, 57(2), 124–141.

Jones, C. (2007). *Institutional repositories: content and culture in an open access environment*. Oxford, UK: Chandos Publishing.

Lally, A.M. and Dunford, C.E. (2007). Using Wikipedia to extend digital collections. *D-Lib Magazine*, 13(4–5). Retrieved on January 21, 2010 from *http://www.dlib.org/ dlib/may07/lally/05lally.html*

Lessig, L. (2007). Larry Lessig on laws that choke creativity. TED. Retrieved on January 31, 2010 from *http://www .ted.com/talks/larry_lessig_says_the_law_is_strangling_ creativity.html*

Luhrs, E. (2008) MetaDB: A distributed metadata creation tool. Retrieved January 30, 2010 from *http://www. departments.bucknell.edu/isr/DIG/MADLC/MADLC-EricLuhrs.pdf*

Lynch, C. (2003). Institutional Repositories: Essential Infrastructure for Scholarship in the Digital Age. ARL: A Bimonthly Report, no. 266 (February 2003). Retrieved January 27, 2010 from *http://www.arl.org/bm~doc/ br226ir.pdf*

Malenfant, K. (2010). Leading change in the system of scholarly communication: A case study of engaging liaison libarians for outreach to faculty. *College & Research Libraries*, 71, 63-76.

Palmer, C., Teffeau, L., and Newton, M. (2008) Strategies for institutional repository development: A case study of three evolving intiatives. *Library Trends*, 57(2), 142–167.

PREMIS Editorial Committee. (2008). PREMIS data dictionary for preservation metadata. Retrieved on January 20, 2010 from *http://www.loc.gov/standards/premis/v2/premis-2-0.pdf*

Prudlo, M. (2005). E-Archiving: An overview of some repository management software tools. Ariadne, 43. Retrieved January 31, 2010 from *http://www.ariadne.ac.uk/issue43/prudlo/*

Salo, D. (2008). Innkeeper at the roach motel. *Library Trends*, 57(2), 98-123.

Smith, E. (2008). Streaming multimedia for digital libraries and IRs such as DSpace: An introduction. Retrieved January 30, 2010 from *http://www.pskl.us/wp/?p=78*

Springer, M., Dulabahn, B., Michel, P., Natanson, B., Reser, D., Woodward, D., et al. (2008). For the common good: The Library of Congress Flickr pilot project. Washington, DC: Library of Congress. Retrieved on January 21, 2010 from *http://www.loc.gov/rr/print/flickr_report_final.pdf*

Suber, P. (2007). Open access overview. Retrieved January 18, 2010 from *http://www.earlham.edu/~peters/fos/overview.htm*

Trustworthy repositories audit & certification: Criteria and checklist. (2007) Retrieved on January 20, 2010 from *http://www.crl.edu/sites/default/files/attachments/pages/trac_0.pdf*

Walters, T. (2007). Reinventing the Library – How repositories are causing librarians to rethink their professional roles. *portal: Libraries and the Academy*, 7(2), 213–225.

Index